D1399567

EDUCATION IN A
CHANGING WORLD

EDUCATION IN A
CHANGING WORLD

A SYMPOSIUM

EDITED BY

CHARLES HENRY DOBINSON

Essay Index Reprint Series

 BOOKS FOR LIBRARIES PRESS
FREEPORT, NEW YORK

First Published 1951 by Oxford University Press

Reprinted 1970 by arrangement

INTERNATIONAL STANDARD BOOK NUMBER:
0-8369-1801-0

LIBRARY OF CONGRESS CATALOG CARD NUMBER:
78-117783

PRINTED IN THE UNITED STATES OF AMERICA

CONTENTS

Introduction vii
THE EDITOR

1. *The State and Education* 1
   C. R. MORRIS, M.A., Vice-Chancellor, The University of Leeds.

2. *Education in Industry* 18
   R. W. REVANS, M.A., D.PH., Education Officer, The National Coal Board.

3. *Educational Reorganization in Relation to the Social Order* 34
   I. L. KANDEL, M.A., PH.D., LITT.D., LL.D., Professor Emeritus, Teachers' College, Columbia University; Professor of American Studies in the University of Manchester.

4. *Intellectual Freedom and the Schools* . . . 47
   J. F. WOLFENDEN, C.B.E., Vice-Chancellor, The University of Reading; lately Headmaster of Shrewsbury School.

5. *The International Aspect of Education* . . . 63
   SIR JOHN MAUD, K.C.B., C.B.E., Permanent Secretary, The Ministry of Education.

6. *The Scientific Background to Educational Change* . 84
   REX KNIGHT, M.A., Professor of Psychology in the University of Aberdeen.

7. *Some fundamental Questions raised by Education's New Role* 105
   L. A. REID, M.A., Professor of the Philosophy of Education in the University of London.

8. *Constructive Change in Education. A Synthesis* . 123
   C. H. DOBINSON, M.A., B.SC., Reader in Education in the University of Oxford.

INTRODUCTION

WHY this title? Surely there has never been a static world? 'Time changes the nature of the whole world', wrote Lucretius, 'and all things pass on from one condition to another and nothing continues like to itself, all things quit their bounds.' Change, then, paradoxically is no change for the world; it is the persistence of its most fundamental process. So, it may be said, teaching and learning have always been 'Education in a changing world'.

But rate of change, is that established too? Clearly the experience of the last few years has shown that it is not; rather it seems as though the winter-long fermentation that charges the heady wine were now being accomplished in a few moments before our eyes. We live in a world in which a whole group of overwhelmingly significant changes have occurred in less than half a century. Man struggling age-long against Nature has won the essential victory. Not quite predictable, but with grudging obedience, Caliban is now the slave and man can call the tune. It may be harmony that he calls or the cacophony that preludes destruction. It may be the music of a Garden of Eden where food and people are proportionate, or a spreading desert overtaking a Malthusian famine. It may be a world rejoicing in its diversity or a world cowering beneath storm clouds of fear worse than primitive man knew in his animistic cave.

In the words of A. J. Toynbee:

Our Western 'know-how' has unified the whole world in the literal sense of the whole habitable and traversable surface of the globe; and it has inflamed the institutions of War and Class, which are the two congenital diseases of civilisation, into utterly fatal maladies. . . . We have to abolish War and Class—and abolish them now—under pain, if we flinch or fail, of seeing them win a victory over man which, this time, would be conclusive and definitive.

The same idea was expressed by Sir Raymond Priestley, Vice-Chancellor of Birmingham University, in 1945 when he said 'Unless we can considerably step up the moral ideas of humanity within a single generation civilisation as we know it may be doomed'.

Clearly, then, if this challenge to humanity is to be met, it must be met in the field of education—the total education of mind and spirit. Old problems must be seen with new eyes discerning their inwardness, and our children must grow up with new attitudes towards one another and towards the young men and women of other nations, other races, and other colours.

Too often we learn only through suffering. During the humiliating years of occupation Frenchmen searched their hearts and found much to condemn in their system of education, still dominated by the bookish tradition of the Jesuits and the rigid controls of Napoleon. The great far-seeing plan for the reform of education known as the Langevin plan has resulted. The need for changes in the educational system has been similarly recognized among other nations. In this country also the inadequacy of our pre-war education became clearer under the impact of warfare that demands the utmost intellectual contribution of man, woman, and adolescent. At the same time the part played in our salvation by the reforms of the 1902 Education Act became more apparent and this dual vision and other factors produced the Education Act of 1944.

Since the end of the war in 1945 some of the developments made possible under this Act have gradually been taking shape. Many of these have been greeted with general approval; in other cases grave doubts have been expressed. Are not some of the means of fulfilment ill-chosen? Will they, in fact, achieve their object? Are they not destroying what is known to be good while pursuing will-of-the-wisp something better? Have the philosophical fundamentals been given enough consideration before the practical steps are taken? Are we going in the right direction? Have we any sense of direction at all?

Questions of this kind have been asked and not merely by ancestral voices.

It was to give the considered answer of some of the recognized authorities in the educational world that the series of lectures from which this book results was given in the University of Oxford during the academic year 1949–50.

1

The State and Education

C. R. MORRIS

SINCE the Education Act of 1944 the State has set as its aim to provide for every child an education suited to its 'age, abilities, and aptitudes'. This is undoubtedly intended to be a positive aim.

In the early stages of progressive legislation the State accommodated itself, in idea as well as in practice, to an established educational order. There were schools available for children whose parents wished to take advantage of them, and some, of course, were better and some were worse. There was a not unnatural tendency for the expensive schools to be better and the less expensive schools not so good. There were exceptions no doubt; but for the most part the children of well-to-do parents tended to receive a better education than the children of the poor. The first step for the State was, speaking very generally, to take the schools as they found them and to open them progressively more and more to suitable children without regard to what the parents could afford. Even when it came to provide schools of its own the State conformed substantially to the existing pattern.

The cheapest schools aimed at providing a minimum training, and that minimum was very low. As the country became more intensively industrial, and industry became more elaborate, the minimum education itself became higher. But for a large proportion of its boys and girls the State was still wedded to the idea of providing a minimum, and withdrawing them for as short a period as possible from their working life.

In the more expensive schools, though there were apt until very lately to be surprising touches of barbarism, something much more ambitious was aimed at. School life was comparatively long, and the aim was to give an all-round education such as would enable the boy to acquit himself creditably in any (no doubt comparatively high and responsible) state of life to which it might please God to call him. No one knew what a boy or girl might be called to do; but whatever it might be, and at whatever time of life, he or she might reasonably expect to find that the necessary basic training, of intellect and of character, had been received at school. The highest recommendation for a place of education was that the bishops, judges, or proconsuls among its old pupils (who had of course not been elevated to their very responsible positions until their school-days were some thirty or forty years behind them) should say that they owed their virtues and their success largely to their school. This idea—that the future was unknown and a boy must be prepared for anything—was carried so far that it was insisted that education was to be had at its best by the study of 'useless' subjects —useless in themselves, but supposedly chosen for their value in training the mind to face with address, good judgement, and courage any task that might come his way.

Here the intervention of the State led to some change in the idea. As established schools were opened more and more, through the action of the State, to the children of the less secure and self-confident classes—and even more as the State came to extend this type of education by providing additional schools in this *genre* itself—there was a marked tendency to give more anxious attention to short-term results, and to consider less the long-term aims. A school came to be judged more by the number of its university scholarships, and less by the number of bishops and cabinet ministers among its old boys. There was an increasing clamour for useful subjects, and a school took great pride in earning golden opinions from its ex-pupils' first employers. The idea may have been that if a boy does his first job well, the rest of his life will look after itself. Or alternatively perhaps nobody was looking beyond the short term. After another great war it is sometimes difficult to do justice even to our own ideas of two or three decades ago.

Even so, however, although in the higher schools the action of the State caused some change in the pre-existent pattern, it was a modification and a compromise, and not a launching out into something fundamentally new, based upon a different idea. The traditional pattern still held its ground, stronger on balance than the modifying influences. It did not change because there was nothing in the social philosophy of the reformers which called for such change.

The social concept was that of a community which would be safest and most contented if a certain number of its members received a generous and liberal education, while the rest of its members got to work at their trades as soon as possible, remaining at school only long enough to receive a minimum essential training. Nobody troubled himself very much with the question whether nature had been over-lavish in her provision and had brought into being an unnecessarily large number of children who would have 'profited' by the higher, liberal education, and whose potentialities were therefore being 'wasted' or lost to the world through so very short a schooling. Individual cases were noticed, as everyone knows; and the State devoted itself, by bits and pieces, to the work of human salvage. Broadly speaking it confined itself to this limited aim. The age of planning and of statistics had not yet arrived. If there was thought at all about overall numbers, and the overall distribution of abilities in the population, it was taken for granted that there were an appropriate number of unworthy pupils in the higher schools who could be excluded to make room for the unprivileged who ought to have their chance.

Now all this has changed, and the State has committed itself to a new starting-point. Every child has certain abilities and aptitudes, and these can be discovered. The child must be given the education which suits his abilities and aptitudes; if it is not, there will be a waste which the State is determined not to allow.

It may be said that this is an act of high faith; that it is casting bread upon the waters in the grand manner. Who can foresee that if every boy and girl is given the education which suits his abilities and aptitudes, all those boys and girls will afterwards fit together into a social pattern which will make the community a going concern? Who can be sure that there will continue, in the life of a mechanized age, to be jobs in which the undergifted can pay a fair return for their expensive education? Who can guarantee that there will be satisfying openings for all the gifted few? But parents have not been stopped in the past by such fears; and the State does not propose to pay too much heed to them now.

May we now turn to the question—'How far do our educational traditions and our accumulated experience make us competent to achieve this ideal?' Have we a clear idea of the kind of education which will best suit the aptitudes and abilities of the different sorts of children? Are the necessary techniques at our disposal? Have we a sufficiently clear idea of what the different sorts of children *are*?

The last question may appear to be fundamental and very difficult. Yet both parents and schools are in substantial agreement on the following: that there are some children who should have full-time schooling up to the age of about sixteen years, others who should remain at school until about eighteen years, and others again who should have a school and college education up to twenty-one or twenty-two years of age or later. In addition, it is widely agreed that boys and girls of the first class, while they should begin plying their trade in workshop or field at about sixteen years, should have part-time schooling in addition for another two years or so.

Cynics say that these types are put forward because such a classification suits the existing educational set-up. But in this particular matter the existing set-up seems to have come to be what it is because the different types of children are what they are; because, that is to say, the evidence in experience for this broad classification is compelling. It must be true, as the idealist argues, that during the years of vital development the young human being will grow up better in a school, which is especially designed to aid his growth, than he will in a factory which is designed to produce as many goods as possible at the lowest possible cost. And everybody will agree that all the years up to twenty-one or twenty-two are years of vital development. But educational experience shows that to keep a boy at school after he ceases to be happy and zealous in school life is usually to do him positive harm; and the same experience has convinced almost everyone that it takes a very good school indeed, exploiting every possible interest and activity from games and bee-keeping to school councils or school parliaments, to keep some children profiting from full-time school education much beyond the age of sixteen.

This does not mean—or at least it is hoped and believed that it will not mean—that the education of such children will stop at this age. But it does mean that they will only benefit from further schooling if they are permitted for their main activity to 'go to work', to learn and ply their trades. We need not here and now seek the reasons for this. We need only observe that it appears to be established as a broad truth by a wealth of experience, both of parents and of schoolmasters and that it seems unlikely that any further study will upset it.

If we accept this rough classification as a lesson of experience, one thing will immediately strike us. Almost without exception, the expensive kinds of education have concentrated their attention on providing for boys and girls who call for the longer schooling. In those institutions where educators have a reasonable opportunity to 'let themselves go', where they have been able to aim at the best with some measure of disregard of outside opinion or of cost, the pupils who occupied the centre of the stage have been, and have been intended to be, of the types that will benefit from a long education. And, broadly speaking, the schools which might have built up a body of knowledge and valuable experience by giving their main attention to the needs of other types of children have been subject to the severest financial limitations. They have learned a very great deal, so to speak, about what is 'the best that you can get for tenpence halfpenny', but very little about what is the best that can be done without regard to cost.

How much does our tradition teach us about the intermediate class—those boys and girls who should probably leave

school and get 'to work' at about eighteen? It is a common-
place to say that our public schools and grammar schools—
which have certainly been much admired abroad for some of
their qualities—have really concentrated on an education supposedly suitable for those pupils who are going to go on to a
university. But even when this was most true, the schools
depended for the continuance of their existence on large
numbers of parents whose boys and girls would leave school
at seventeen or eighteen but who were nevertheless convinced
that the education provided, though not primarily designed
for their children, would suit their children extremely well.
At any rate they thought it would be very much better than
any alternative way of spending the years concerned which was
really practicable.

Actually these schools turned aside and paid a great deal of
attention to this kind of boy and girl; so much so that they have
sometimes been severely criticized in the present century by
visitors from overseas for paying insufficient attention to the
things of the intellect. Indeed, of recent years many of these
schools have been more successful with boys and girls who
were *not* very intellectually inclined than with pupils who were
due to proceed to the university. This was not because the
course of studies pursued was particularly well designed for
pupils of this type, but because the games and other activities,
which *were* especially good for them, were stronger features of
the school life than were the formal studies. In spite, therefore,
of the strident differences of opinion about curricula which are
such a bewildering feature of our educational world to-day, it
may be said with some confidence that our English educational
tradition teaches us a good deal about the kind of education
which suits the abilities and aptitudes of this middle kind of
child.

By the same token our tradition can give us a good start in
working out a more ambitious education than we have hitherto
sought to provide for those children who will 'go to work' at
the age of sixteen. It teaches us that a full education is more
than intellectual training or the pursuit of academic studies.

There are two other elements at least to be considered, the technical skills and the aesthetic emotions. As regards the latter, though there is much justice in the prevalent view that English schools—at any rate boys' schools—are predominantly philistine in their influence, many have undoubtedly done fine work in this direction. In parts of our society, in spite of the facilities offered by broadcasting, boys and girls have almost no chance of discovering their aesthetic selves at all in the home circle; their only hope lies in the school or the college. No one can doubt that there are immense possibilities of development here.

When we turn to the technical skills it is necessary to make a distinction. No school, when it gives a boy opportunity to practise a special skill, is in the narrow sense teaching him that special skill for its own sake. The specially applied skill of hand and eye which will make the man a quick and efficient worker in his trade will be learned later in the workshop; and it will need a degree of concentration and practice over a long period of time, such as no one would encourage or allow for a boy at school. Rather a boy will be encouraged in his education to try several skills, so as to have some acquaintance with others than that which will eventually be his own. This will not only help him to gauge his own aptitudes and choose his calling wisely, but it will also throughout his life have a value of its own. Again, a boy may well be going, in his after-employment, to play some part in an elaborately mechanized process, or himself to use an extremely complicated machine. But no schoolmaster seeks to train him to use such a machine while at school; he rather teaches him the use and virtue of the simple tools and simple operations out of which the elaborately mechanized machines and processes are developed. The aim is not only to train the hand and the eye, but to cause the boy to reflect and to *understand*; and in greater or in less measure the aim is achieved.

Even manual skills then, as they are taught at school, in some measure touch the intellect; and the same is true of the arts. If a school enables a boy to come to enjoy listening to music, or looking at pictures, or painting or playing an instrument himself, it does so partly because in after-life the boy may derive much pleasure, and sometimes more than pleasure, from continuing these activities. But it does so also because, in the atmosphere of the school, these things will make him *think*; he will explain and discuss with his friends and with his masters, and will in some degree at least seek to answer intellectual questions. Not in very high degree no doubt; the poet and the painter are not usually addicted to logical precision, and the craftsman does not as a rule press his philosophical inquiries beyond a certain point. But the intellect is stirred into action, often most quickly and directly in pupils who for school purposes are not very intellectual. And this activity of thought, though it has arisen almost as a kind of by-product and in passing, has a value in its own right.

It may be then that we can see in dim outline a satisfactory kind of education for the less intellectually interested children —a certain minimum of academic studies, some practice in technical skills, some opportunity to experience the arts, together with the various kinds of activities and pursuits which have been associated with the success of our system in the development of character. If in deference to the present anti-academic fashion we should lean too far backwards and cut out too much of the 'academic', we shall still have a strong and vigorous course of schooling, and there should be no difficulty in remedying the defect as experience brings it to notice. Here again, in a comparatively unploughed field, our tradition should bring us to success.

We may fortify ourselves in this conclusion by considering more closely what we expect of education. It is true that the great philosophers of the ages differ about its definition. But we are being taught again daily by the changes in our time that some of the things which have been in the past so much taken for granted that they are not mentioned are the most important things, even though to-day they can by no means be taken for granted.

In any case we dare not, as practical teachers, shirk the issue of determining as clearly as we can what our education is aiming at. For one thing we are all agreed that something is done to children in the first few years of their lives that can never be undone. In some respects they are almost automata for the rest of their lives under the control of attitudes fixed in these early years; in some respects they are in conscious, almost in conscientious, revolt against these influences; in other matters they are hampered by some vacuum in themselves, which might have been filled in early childhood, by the atrophy of capacities and potentialities which were by no means predestined to wither and die. If it is true, and I think it is, that it is better for everybody—for the child and for the nation—that education should, in the most important things, be achieved by a partnership between the home and the school, then it is of the greatest importance that this partnership should start when the home is the more powerful partner at the nursery-school age. Professionals who have given their lives to the study and practice of how to get the best out of children should have their share of these very early years. And it is essential, for the proper treatment of this vital age, to have a clear idea of the direction in which education as a whole is to go.

Let there be no mistake about it, the things which are determined at the very beginnings of life are among the most important things. The teacher whose experience has been with other ages knows from that experience how very great can be the development of boys and girls in those later years with which he is concerned. But he also knows that in the most fundamental matters, of sentiment, of emotional poise, of habit of mind, of approach to God and man, what he can do at the later age is limited by the existence of a hardened core within the personality which it is then beyond his power to change. There is nothing new in this doctrine; but its comparative neglect in practice, especially by the State, is at the root of many of the faults of which we are most conscious in our education to-day.

It has been customary for some time to condemn our British education rather severely for its defects on the moral side. It does not produce the good men or the good citizens, we say, that we might fairly expect. In the past we have been credited, in the judgement of the world at large, with outstanding success in the training of character. We are philistines, we are told, and do not know how to educate the sensibility; we are practical men, and other nations of western Europe have been our superiors in developing the young intellect. But in the training of character we are unsurpassed, so it has often been said. The Spartans and the Romans knew a thing or two in this field, but they failed to give their citizens a moral fibre which would pass with credit the test of a long period of service abroad, and they failed to maintain the supply of first-class politicians and public servants. On both these criteria our system has been given much credit.

But judgement to-day, especially at home, is not happy about this. Our pre-eminence as moral educators, we tell ourselves, if ever it existed, has gone. It is true that we do not always seem very clear in our minds about what is wrong. Sometimes we say that all that people care about is money; but then at other times we say that the money incentive has failed in our country, as compared for instance with America. Again, we sometimes say that in our generation we do not care for the future, but live too much in the day. Yet I suppose we are showing more effective care for the old and for the young than any society before us—and this not only by social action but by personal devotion as well. As every teacher knows, there are more parents taking the greatest pains and making high sacrifices for their children's education than ever before; and there are probably more people doing voluntary public work than ever before. At other times, we charge ourselves with caring only for the interests of our own families or our own class. Yet in the long history of the world no great society has conscientiously and consistently shared out food and other necessities in short supply as we have done in the last ten years —and this, not merely with the consent but largely by the compulsion of popular opinion.

We are not in the Victorian tradition. We do not approach

the estimation of ourselves and of our institutions assuming that we are a great people and have great institutions, and merely seeking to fill in in detail what it is that makes for greatness in us and in them. We are children of Marx and of Freud; we see magnified our own feet of clay. We approach the study of anything and everything taking it for granted that it could be very much better than it is, and that we could make it so if we would. Even if our own personal lives, or the national life, in some regards look fair upon the surface, we assume that probing will show terrible things underneath. We blame ourselves accordingly, and of course our faith in ourselves has suffered. An intense degree of self-castigation never has been, and never will be, productive of heroic virtue.

Look on this picture and on that, as teachers say, and judge for yourselves. When we looked at Hitler, and then back at ourselves, we for the time being concentrated on our own virtues and advantages, by contrast with something whose principles we condemned and hated; and we fought a vigorous, not to say heroic, war for our own way of life. It is perhaps significant, however, of our age that we encouraged ourselves at the time with thoughts not so much of what we were as of what we might be, not of our actual virtues and achievements but of the possibilities which these seemed to open before us.

We need not now pursue farther the question of what is wrong with our time and generation. We have gone far enough to see what are the things which we most look for in a good education. Traditionally there has always been a strong strain of realism in our aims and hopes. We have sought to prepare men and women to live, and to expect themselves to live, at a moral level which was neither that of the saint nor that of the fool or the selfish hedonist, but was well on the right side of half-way. We have expected our schools and colleges to make us wish to put more into the pool than we took out; to accept the responsibilities laid upon us by our natural gifts and other advantages; to do many things with credit, and one thing as well as we are capable of doing; to act from desire for human welfare and not from fear; and to acquire, according to our abilities, the self-control, endurance, and intellectual acumen and enterprise necessary to this way of life.

This programme differs from the aims as given by great philosophers only by setting the sights too low. There is nothing in it about beauty and the arts; nothing about truth and pure reason; nothing about the love of God or religion. If the truth be told we have traditionally been tempted to leave it to other agencies to see to these things. But if in our education we have aimed rather low, we have been thought by many to come very near in the past to hitting the mark we aimed at. And it is as compared with this restricted success in days gone by that we commonly regard ourselves as failing in the present.

We ought to look for a moment at the political implications of our educational practice. Our schools and colleges have played their part, German scholars and others have frequently told us, in producing a people of great political maturity. By this they mean that while we can be swept away by moments of passion—of sudden hatred, fear, or wild flights of ill-grounded hope—we come back quite quickly as a people to remembering and weighing the main facts and values; and we have great faith in institutions which encourage us to do this, even at times when circumstances make second thinking somewhat fraught with danger. A well-tried institution is not hastily scrapped with us, and a well-tried policy not abandoned without a careful review of its successes in the past and the presumed reasons for them. There was a time between the wars when this so-called political maturity seemed to be failing; when our belief in British traditions in politics was weakening, and it seemed that a general apathy might open the door to something unpredictable. But the signs are, for what they are worth, that this moment has passed; that there is conviction again, if not passion, behind the political parties, and that there is, in the traditional way, enough and yet not too much of conflict between their differing policies.

These considerations may leave us, I think, with a fair feeling of optimism. We are building without doubt a new age in national education; but the new system when it is built will be found, not to 'have growed up one dark night', but to have emerged from an old tradition. But as educators our clients are now not the parents, but the State; and we have to allow for a differently balanced concept of what is required.

The parents, when they were in control, encouraged a high ideal in the determinant part of the system. They sought something which was more than worthy of respect; and the State has not done ill in seeking, in very large measure, to provide for the many what parents who could were entirely willing to pay for the few. In some degree, no doubt, the State was bound to fail in this; because in *some* degree what was given to the few could only be given so long as it was given to the few only. But over a wider field good education, like love, 'differs from golden clay'; and it has been possible for democracy to reap the benefit of the experience gained under the older system.

In some measure the State was bound to call a different tune. Like good parents, it commits itself, without too much counting of the cost and sacrifice involved, to giving a chance to every boy and every girl; it is committed to giving the education which suits the individual's aptitudes and abilities, without stopping to ask too much whether the community could have gone on its way to security and prosperity with less well-educated citizens. Let us do everything we can, the State seems to say, and give the young their full chance. This is the language of faith and of affection, rather than the language of close reckoning of small gains and losses.

But while thus aiming to give every individual his full opportunity, to open the door for him to the highest achievements of which he is capable, the State is bound to be more affected by social concepts than the parent used to be. For one thing there is a long tradition in this country that what is paid for by public money should be fairly distributed. In the middle stages of the growth of the new system the application of this concept of fair distribution can be cramping. The principle can take the negative form of unwillingness to give the best to *anyone* at a stage when it cannot be given to *everyone*. This attitude may cause the best to disappear, and the secret to be lost of how to produce it. But in the long run, in the ideal, it seems that there may be no indefeasible conflict between equity and high quality. The principle of education according to aptitudes and abilities may in the issue be accepted as meeting the demands of fairness. There need then be nothing in the way of the pursuit of the best for everyone.

Of course some things are made more difficult for the educator by emphasis on the principles which the State puts in the forefront. Democratic virtue is more difficult to educate for than aristocratic virtue. Take initiative, for instance. It is easy to induce a boy to surrender himself to a difficult discipline of self-training on the ground that he will have to show *outstanding* initiative, much more initiative than other people. It is less easy on the ground that *everybody* ought to develop his capacity for initiative, as he ought to develop *all* his capacities. The social concepts of democracy tend to make it more difficult for education to sharpen the finer edges of human capacities. *Noblesse oblige* has always been found a most powerful argument with youth, and by no means a despicable one; but it has been by no means easy to find an unexceptionally democratic form in which it could be used.

Yet it will be fatal to democracy if it is afraid of quality. The educator is of all people the most aware of natural inequalities in his daily work. The doctrine that these inequalities are only differences, and that every man can be perfect in his own way is good Christianity and good sense; but it is not easily compatible with ordinary social ideas. The idea dies hard that some individuals are more valuable than others; it lies deep in almost universal judgements about the real world. The poet is felt to be 'higher type' than the violinist, the statesman than the administrator, the craftsman than the mechanic, and so on. The boy whose 'aptitudes and abilities' keep him at school and college till twenty-one is apt to be regarded as a nobler work of God than he whose natural endowment makes him happier in a workshop or office after the age of sixteen.

Christianity has taught us that all are equal in the sight of God and should be equal in the sight of the Christian man.

But in the minds of most people this 'equality' is banished to the realm of some mystical world and not accepted in the actual life of every day. So long as this is so there is a clear temptation for the State to shrink from encouraging differences, which are in practice honoured on every hand as inequalities, and to make the school pattern operate to tone down features which might appear to be obstacles to social unity.

It does not seem that this reluctance has much to do with the differences between political parties. It is deeply infused in a philosophy of educational progress built up, in the way of our country, as the result of stresses in practical experience, rooted in faiths which are fundamental to our love of free institutions, and fixed in detail by the determination to face inexorable facts. One party has one part of the pattern nearer to its heart, and the other party another part; one party would take more risks than the other with educational standards and with the economic balance-sheet of gains and losses from increased expenditure on the nation's schools. But these are not great differences; and the pattern of the picture is well defined, with its encouraging features and its dangers, whatever may be the ups and downs of the opposing parties.

The reluctance I have referred to is not diminished .by the sense that a system of education which favours the highest development of high abilities tends in some degree towards a hardening of class differences and the conservation of class structures. Intellectual interests are not naturally fostered by the common life of an industrial community; yet without them the higher education of the individual is not possible. The higher learning and real research calls for devotion in the student, indeed for self-dedication. There must be powerful incentives, and also strength of character. The struggle in the world of education to-day is not to find the techniques for giving every advantage to the suitable and willing student, but to find the techniques *for fostering the will in the student*. In the parts of society where this is at present most successfully achieved, it is achieved by the home rather than by the school. In the immense number of cases where it cannot be done by the home, there is still a probability, in spite of the tremendous efforts of the schools, that it will not be done at all. To make a real scholar, or a real researcher, out of a boy or girl from a home that can do little or nothing to help, requires twice the work from the school. With most of the boys and girls who come to high success, half the job is still done before ever they enter the school gates. The advances that have been made in the last forty years in methods of presenting to pupils the established subjects have been quite spectacular. But we have barely started upon the task of learning how to enable the boy or girl without home advantages to acquire the interests and stamina required to stay the pace of the higher education.

I have known university teachers who have thought, from their practical experience in teaching, that in the higher flights of scholarship a girl must be half as good again as her brother in ability to do as well as he. I should certainly venture the opinion that under the present conditions a boy from an unhelpful home needs twice the ability required by his contemporary who has every home advantage.

This is not an insurmountable obstacle; it is only a challenge, if a very difficult one. If we give as much attention in the next forty years to this problem of the liberation of interests and energies as has been given in the past forty to the techniques of subject teaching, the challenge will be well met. And if it *is* met this fear of the hardening of class structures will be more unfounded than it is to-day. Even the *prospect* of success in this matter may lead us to be less nervous in the determination not to waste the natural supply of intellectual ability in the nation.

Apart from the sheer economic necessity to do this, we with our traditions should never be happy or comfortable living in a world which it did not take all sorts to make. We do not enjoy monotony; we have a marked liking for 'characters' and 'personalities'. It is true that we have frequently in the past been charged with making unwarranted sacrifices in the interests of conformity to a pattern. Our great schools have been thought to be very hard on the artist and the intellectual; they have been powerful influences pressing all types towards the normal. And foreign critics have told us that our social cohesiveness, and the attractively loose structure of society which this makes possible, is all of a piece with the ethos of our schools. The lion can lie down with the lamb with us, at any rate in most circles; and we may be thankful for it.

But on the whole, in spite of this strong strand in our tradition of worship of the normal, we have not, in the higher flights of education, been afraid of excellence or of the full exploitation of high ability. In much of public life at home, and in imperial government overseas, we have pinned our faith to a rigorous examination system, which may not yet have run its course with us. We have shown our confidence in brains—at any rate in brains as moulded by our British schools and colleges. It would on the whole be against our tradition to be unwilling to allow the intellectually gifted boy or girl to go his own way, at his own pace, through fear that it would make him too 'different' for the rest of his life. And we should certainly pay a very great price if we did so.

It has always been urged against democracy that it fears excellence; and the democrat has usually replied with Pericles that the truth is the contrary. Certainly it is not democracy which fears to take risks; it accepts risks with both hands from a sure faith in the best in human nature. But in educational matters we have undoubtedly before us a big test. Are we willing to go all the way that our educational traditions and techniques would enable us to go? Are we prepared to give to every child in full confidence the education which is suitable to his abilities and aptitudes? To *every* child—not only to those who approach the normal, not only to those of such low endowment as to be specially vulnerable or dangerous; but also to those of high ability who are capable of exacting interests and pursuits, and of high service to the community. No parent would hesitate in regard to his own family, however divergent the natural gifts of his children. And in this our democratic State need not lag behind the good parent.

2

Education in Industry

R. W. REVANS

MY task is to discuss education in industry, and to stress, if I can, the importance of education in establishing and maintaining that harmony between all those engaged in producing and distributing the world's wealth that is known as good industrial relations. In some ways my assignment is not an easy one, for the status of education in the eyes of the industrialist is changing at the present moment; some firms are quick to see that in the educationist they have a valuable ally: the attitude of others remains more traditional. Although industry and trade are both more widely recognizing that the efficiency of production is in the end merely the efficiency of the producers, there still lurks a fear that the processes of education may bring forth some undesirable by-products. We must all remember that, in addition to ordered thinking having its dangers, education has a strong literary tradition; it has been designed more in the interests of those who write letters about things than of those who do them; it has not infrequently tended to train for responsible administrative positions men who have either positively despised the skill of the engineer, or deliberately kept themselves in genteel ignorance of the risks of the market and the exchange.

We cannot deny that there is a cleavage between the academic, on the one hand, and the banausic on the other; we see it in the veiled incompatibility between the intellectual and the trade-union wings of the Labour Party; it turns up inside education itself as the contrast between the university and the technical college, between the grammar school and the technical secondary school. These are all examples of an antithesis between scribe and artisan that enters deeply into the whole of human society; sometimes it appears as a downright class distinction, the manual worker providing by his labour the leisure and the opportunity for the scholar to be trained as the new industrial captain; already one senses a fear among the working class that the great expansion of the universities in recent years, however democratically achieved, may merely be the silent reinforcement of the bosses. But the true antithesis is that between fulfilment and survival; between the enrichment of human life and experience, on the one hand, and our physical survival on the other. For liberal education is, or should be, concerned with those achievements of the mind and spirit that men will always recognize to be great; industry and trade, on the other hand, are mainly concerned with the materials and services of existence; the difference goes deeply into our national consciousness: only a commercial nation, groping to express its amused contempt for things of the mind, could have given birth to the word 'highbrow'.

This contrast between fulfilment and survival, this ambiguity in the true relation between education and industry, may be read in the oldest records of humanity; the workers of Rome and Egypt equally identified education with the 'literocracy'; even over three thousand years ago education was regarded as the means of escape from toil, just as, until quite recently, it was the best way from the coal-face to the pulpit or the desk. The first of these passages I take from Toynbee's *Study of History*; it is advice given by an Egyptian parent to his schoolboy son.

I have seen him that is beaten: thou art to set thy heart on books. I have beheld him that is set free from forced labour: behold, nothing surpasseth books. The stone mason seeketh for work in all manner of hard stone. When he hath finished it his arms are destroyed and he is weary. The field worker, his reckoning endureth for ever; he too is wearier than can be told. The weaver in his workshop, he fareth more ill than any woman. His thighs are on his belly and he breatheth no air. Let me tell thee further how it fareth with the fisherman. Is not his work on the river where it is mixed with the crocodiles? Behold there is no calling that is without a director, except that of the scribe, and he is the director.

The second illustration is from Ecclesiasticus.

The wisdom of a learned man cometh by opportunity of leisure. How can he get wisdom who holdeth the plough, that driveth oxen and is occupied in their labours, and whose talk is of bullocks? ... So every carpenter that laboureth night and day. ... The smith also sitting at his work and the potter turning the wheel about with his feet. ... All these trust in their hands. Without these cannot a city be inhabited. They shall not be sought for in public counsel, nor sit high in the congregation: they shall not sit in the judge's seat nor understand the sentence of judgment. But they will maintain the state of the world and all their desire is in the work of their craft.

We can find, in modern times, similar examples of the divergence between the practical outlook of technology and trade, on the one hand, and the enduring classical and literary outlook of the educationist on the other. The *Spens Report*, published in 1938, advised us to set up technical high schools as equal alternatives to the traditional grammar schools. It was not only the industrialists who had become alarmed by the success of the grammar schools in draining the nation's talent into literary occupations, and leaving the less able pupils to enter industry; our system of public education had tended to make the clerk and the typist more important in the eyes of the nation than the artisan and the nurse. In the words of the Spens report itself:

A careful study of the present position has led us to the belief that the existing arrangements for the whole-time education of boys and girls above the age of eleven in England and Wales have ceased to correspond with the actual structure of modern society and with the economic facts of the situation.

The spirit of this is now written into the Education Act, 1944, although as long ago as 1936 the Essex Education Committee had persuaded the Board of Education, as it then was, to allow them to open the first technical high school in the country. It was one object of this school to determine how far a study of modern industry and trade could take its place in the curriculum as suitably as a study of Shakespeare or Napoleon; and, although the school captured the imagination of local industrialists, it did not teach, and was never designed to teach, manual trades; it was not there merely to equip boys to work in local garages.

There are still some who acknowledge with misgiving the study of science and technology; there is still a feeling in many universities that the only true education is that which deals with our heritage of the scholastic and the academic. In his testament, *Crisis in the University*, Sir Walter Moberly says this of the growth of scientific and engineering studies at Oxford:

They (the scientists) were not really admitted to the Brahmin Caste. 'Stinks' had not the same rank in the hierarchy as *Literae Humaniores*. Yet if industrialism and democracy are the outstanding and significant forces in the modern world, no philosophy of life or of education, which gives to them only a secondary place and a subsidiary function, can hope to convince.

There are many who would repeat that science and technology are merely a service to the means of our survival, while the *Literae Humaniores* are concerned with our ultimate values; that it is Hollywood on the one hand against the *Summa Theologiae* on the other; that while we admit that science and industry to-day can produce for us *Henry V* in Glorious Technicolour, it was only the spirit of the Elizabethan writers that could have given the work to the world in the first place. But these are dangerous subjects to choose for dialectics; if we are dubious about the place of Mr. J. Arthur Rank in the temple of eternity, we should not deny a prominent one to William Caxton. George Stephenson and Lord Lister were, in the final analysis, only technicians; nobody would, presumably, pretend on that account that they had done less for the happiness of mankind than Goethe or Cézanne, whose appeal is from one imagination to another. The danger is that we do not see the nobility of our technical triumphs, that we apply them to worthless and destructive ends, and that they are not acknowledged to be great by virtue of the freedom that they might give to men to become great. Here again education must, as it were, be waiting in the outfield; of what use is it to free people from unnecessary labour, if they forthwith offer themselves to commercialized time-wasting, deliberately organized as such?

Let us first consider liberal education. We need not spend long upon it, not because a scale of ultimate values is unimportant, but because it is clearly of no concern to industry, as distinct from an industrial society, to provide liberal education. It is not for Henry Ford or the Railway Executive to charge their customers with the expense of teaching their employees Greek. That charge should be carried on the education rate. But it is certainly the concern of industry, as well as of an industrial society, to see that those of its employees who want to learn Greek are encouraged to do so. Put in its very lowest terms, we may agree that the musical coalminer denied his violin is a discontented man, and hence a discontented coalminer; perhaps not many miners are musical in this way, but if the majority are not violin players they may have other and more homely ways of expressing themselves that are only seldom given scope. It is for the local education authority, the Workers' Educational Association, the Extra-Mural Board, and similar bodies to provide this scope; it is the business of industry to encourage its employees to respond, and, to a reasonable degree, to give them the chance of doing so. In the coal industry, which provides itself with a statutory fund to advance the welfare of the miners, it is now the policy of the Miners' Welfare Commission to put their several hundred institutes at the service of the education authorities so that they and the miners may use them to stage intelligent recreation, shared equally with the bakers and candlestick-makers as well. I do not think there is much future scope for leisure time activities run by individual firms as such, except where the single firm is so large as to employ a majority of the local population; colliery bands are examples. But in my view it is misconceived to attempt to engender good 'industrial relations' inside a firm by simply subsidizing the production of oratorios or by fostering mock parliaments; the true understanding that should exist between workers and management is an organic sympathy arising from the work itself. All other bonds are shadows; Gilbert and Sullivan choruses will never shout down the whispers of industrial discontent.

We now come to the second principal subject. Those fields of education in which industry is most at home are, naturally enough, mainly occupied with purely technical instruction; by this we mean the organized efforts of experienced men to communicate their technical knowledge and skill to others. We must not underrate the importance of this, but it is comforting to be able to say that it is a relatively easy task. It is easy because its objectives ought to be clear. If one wants to produce an artificer able to perform a particular job one can do so with reasonable success, simply because one knows what is wanted. His job can be specified, and we know sufficient about the processes of learning and the art of teaching to train him up to any reasonable standard. But I do not believe that it is primarily the job of industry to organize and provide technical education. It is true that there are some processes for which industry alone has the facilities: setting timber on the coal-face must be taught at the coal-face; as a coal-mine may be a highly dangerous place to work in, the supervision and the instruction must, in the end, fall to the people responsible for the safe conduct of the mine. But, on the whole, fundamental technical instruction is much better given by local education authorities in technical colleges than ever it can be inside industry; it is not a primary function of industry to teach and to train; these activities require a certain attitude of mind, and this does not flourish readily in an organization given over primarily to producing things as quickly and cheaply as possible. A good deal of patience is needed to teach boys ideas of accuracy; the technical processes of industry, which are largely empirical, may never be sufficiently analysed in the workshop for the apprentice to understand which are important parts of an operation and which are not. Although the modern highly mechanized factory cannot afford to dispense with the manual skill of the old-time craftsman, the young man set to work in such a place may never learn systematically the use of the traditional tools. Clearly, it is better that apprentices should be taught to use the file and hacksaw, the soldering iron and the callipers, and to read blue-prints and tables at the technical college, rather than in the productive workshop. In saying this we recognize that technical colleges at the moment are under great pressure; none the less, I believe that the extension of fundamental technical education which this country so badly needs must be made mainly by the local education authorities, and only in special directions by industry itself.

As the demands upon technical education become more specialized, industry, of course, must assume greater responsibility for meeting them. Local authorities may teach the generation and distribution of power, or the principles of the design of electric motors. They cannot, however, undertake to train armature winders. This is a job for industry to do on the floor of the workshop. At the same time, the universities and the technical colleges must still retain an important share in the training for industry of senior specialists. The more responsible the post the more essential it is for its occupant to see its wider implications, to understand the impact of his technology upon the social order that it is designed to serve. It is becoming increasingly common for factory managers to be selected from among university graduates, and certainly in the coal-mining industry, where management calls for sociological insight no less than for technical knowledge, it is the policy of the National Coal Board to appoint an increasing number of men with mining degrees.

The efforts that industry is making to-day to attract men from the university may excite suspicion not merely from the workers alone. There are many able managers and directors who shake their heads over these changes. Universities, we are told, tend not to produce men of character. By character, in this context, is presumably meant that iron quality which enabled a man in his early twenties to work, year after year, at evening classes, in order to get a technical qualification without which no promotion was possible. Such a quality brought many great men up from the ranks of industry and commerce; it was self-help of the most exacting kind, and it undoubtedly reserved the final prizes for those of the toughest fibre. But the wastage was enormous. And, moreover, it was always fair to ask whether the quality necessary for survival in this rigorous steeplechase was also that needed to manage and command after the technical qualification had been won. We need not embark upon this question; our answer to the advocates of the hard way is another one. If boys and girls of ability are no longer being driven to leave school at fifteen because there is no longer lack of educational opportunity, but are now staying in the classroom to match their wits against other candidates for university scholarships, it follows that an increasing percentage of the nation's ability finds itself, whether industry approves or not, with its feet on the university threshold. It is in this stream that industry, therefore, must fish for its future talent; it is of no use for industry merely to regard the university man as the long-haired intellectual; and it is, as Moberly points out, for the universities to bring themselves to understand better the industrial world into which their most able products should be launched. The growth of university appointments boards and the endowment by industrial firms of scientific research in university laboratories are each doing much to bring the two traditions together.

We can agree that management to-day demands an understanding of the ideas that men have in their heads, as well as a knowledge of the tools that they hold in their hands. But in addition it is also interesting to ask whether the professional business of management itself can also be taught. Is there a general study of management in its own right as, for example, there is a corpus of teachable knowledge that we call mathematics? And if so, can management as a study be taught, just as, using another example, we can teach the theory of alternating current?

These are questions of profound interest to the educationists lending a hand to industry. We may not be entirely convinced that the claims of management to be recognized as an organic and educational study have yet been fully made out. It was almost a hundred years ago that Cardinal Newman, in his work, *The Scope and Nature of University Education*, told us that the proper business of the university was to develop the judgement; to train the mind rather than to diffuse knowledge; to give a man so wide a view that he could not only use his own knowledge, but could also command that of others. To this extent Newman must be regarded as an early advocate of management education; although there are some who would deny that the judgement developed through, say, literary or historical criticism could be, as Newman implied, transferred to fields other than literature and history.

The art of management is the art of getting people to do things, and although one may analyse management into forecasting, planning, organizing, commanding, co-ordinating, and controlling, each one of these six activities is merely the result of the interplay of a large number of factors, some of which are imperfectly seen, while others are entirely matters of opinion. One may be able to teach many specific techniques, for example, of costing, accounting, factory organization, wage-negotiation, company law, and so forth, but whether one can also teach their orchestration into management, as Newman might be interpreted to suggest, is another matter. One can teach a boy to write, to recognize rhyme and metre, but one cannot teach him to write plays as good as Shakespeare's; one can perhaps organize correspondence courses explaining various cricket strokes, but it is more difficult in this way to teach men to make centuries in Test Matches. Nevertheless, the first essential to any progress in education for management is to create a widespread opinion that managerial problems lend themselves to analytical study, and that from such analysis it may be possible to draw rational conclusions. It is probably true to say that at the present time there is a growing willingness among managers to admit that such analytical study is possible. The field to be investigated is immense; it covers the whole range of relations between workers and their environment, between manager and supervisor, between trade union and directing board. It is inside this field that management must be carried on, and we have yet to lay down the fundamental laws that govern these relations. There are some who call the approach to these studies 'scientific management', or even 'human engineering'. This shows far too narrow a view of what is involved, but if managers like to introduce ideas of order into their work in such mechanical terms no doubt it is better than to remain convinced that managerial skill is some impenetrable mystery. If we discover some of the hidden laws controlling group relations and can, as a result develop codes of instruction which will bring managerial wisdom to men while they are still young and unsoured, then education will have done industry service enough to wipe the old scores off the slate. It has been said many times recently, particularly by some American business men, that nowhere has Britain so much slack to take up as in the management of its industry. We would not pretend that salvation is to be found by changes of attitude in the ranks of management alone; the managed must be as willing to accept new practices as managers should be to try them out. We all know well enough the depressing persistence of restrictive practices, and it is hopeful to see that the study of American productivity which is now being made by British industry takes trade-union leaders, as well as industrial managers, across the Atlantic. In that land of wonders, we are told, the labour unions employ professional consultants to advise them whether or not the firms they work for are being efficiently managed: the American worker apparently understands that it is not merely a matter of getting the best price for his labour in the market that he can; he understands that the market itself must be efficient to make that high price significant.

This disquisition upon education for management, upon the deliberate effort to teach men to make the organization of their factory or counting-house efficient, brings us to our third principal subject. We must ask ourselves how far education can be sociological in its industrial setting, as well as liberal and technical. Aristotle's definition of education should catch our attention at this point. He says, 'In the first place, education aims at producing such a character as will issue in acts tending to promote the happiness of the state; in the second place, it aims at preparing the soul for that right enjoyment of leisure which becomes possible after practical needs have been satisfied.' I have touched upon liberal education to ensure the right enjoyment of leisure, and technical education to fulfil the practical needs. Can there be, as Aristotle suggests, a form of education to make men understand the social, the collective aspects of their work? There seem to be illustrations enough, perhaps more than enough, in history to show that education can be given a strong political or social accent. In Crete and Sparta the boy, like the member of the Hitler-jugend, was taught to prepare himself for death on the battle-field in defence of the State; the educational system of the Jesuits, that could produce a man like Ferdinand of Styria, had powerful social implications; the English public schools were to a large extent the nursery of later imperialism. These efforts were authoritatively pursued by a professional class, armed with powerful educational tools; they achieved habits of social thought that survived for generations. How far ought we to-day to engender collective attitudes in the vast industrial communities that now tend to form States within the modern State? For it is of no use to equip industry with all the fruits of human invention, and to instruct each artisan in their techniques, if the whole are not moved by a sense of common social purpose; any more than it is of use to train each individual soldier in an army to the efficient use of his weapons, unless each and every soldier also has a clear picture of the objective that he is attacking, and the part that he plays alongside his comrades in the attack. It is not unknown for warships that have gone into action without clear instructions to have finished up by sinking their own sister ships; nobody complained that the gunners were inefficient: they were merely firing at the wrong targets. While we do not imply that industrial workers, having no clear picture of the economic battle they are fight-ing, are likely to fall upon one another in the same decisive way, the total waste, day in and day out, that industry may suffer through lacking a common view of a common objective may, in the end, be far more serious than the loss which is caused by mere technical inefficiency or misunderstanding. There are plenty to-day who feel that only by the common purpose of a national war can all the factions of the country be united on one economic front; they speak almost nostalgically of the need for a Dunkirk spirit in the factories and the mines. We often hear, for example, that it is necessary to educate miners or locomotive drivers to the meaning of nationalization. Indeed, there are many who, when scanning the chronicles of the latest industrial stoppages or on reading the latest claims for wage increases, observe that the time has come to educate the workers generally in a sense of their own responsibilities in the precarious quality of the Welfare State and in the economic difficulties of the country. I think that we must inquire what, if anything, the word 'education' means in these circumstances.

Education, as we know it in other forms, however much it may differ from one country or one subject to the next, has at least these three universals. First, a body of teachers; second, a corpus of knowledge or doctrine to be taught; third, a school of disciples, students, or pupils to receive the doctrine at the feet of the teachers. No such three are readily discernible in industry. If one talks of educating the coal industry to the meaning of nationalization one must (assuming that it is the coal-miners who are to be taught) then search for the preceptors and for their texts. It is here that the difficulties arise; the embarrassment is not a shortage of teachers, nor a paucity of doctrine; it is rather a superfluity of both. And if one asked on what authority the teaching was to be given, the miners would claim that it was by their own efforts and those of untold generations of their ancestors that the industry came to be nationalized, and that they have no need of any scholastic hierarchy to interpret to them what those efforts were intended to achieve. Nor, on the other hand, is the National Coal Board short of advisers to tell them how to deal with the miners; to some of these advisers any efforts, including coercion, which, they believe, would cause the men to work, would be regarded as education. There is still a widely expressed opinion that the only true educational medium, or incentive to effort, is the threat of want or unemployment, and that any attempt at rational explanation is, compared with this goad, a mere nothingness.

But, even if we admit reason to have its part, by education in this sense we do not mean mere exhortation, nor the skilful use of different forms of propaganda. We must ask ourselves whether rational conclusions, both about the economic scene and the part of the individual as producer and consumer in that scene, cannot be drawn by intelligent discussion of the issues with which the individual worker is already familiar. The word 'discussion' is used deliberately, because it is essential in such educational efforts that the workers should play a part no less active than those who claim to see the wider social and economic implications. These favoured few might be the members of the Government or their advisers, the directors of industrial boards, men in high positions in the Trade Union movement, and so forth. All of these might claim to read the economic future; all of these might believe that it is their mission to bring a message to the men at the bench or the coal-face. Indeed, the Government already, through the Central Office of Information and other official agencies, is making valiant efforts to encourage the nation to higher productivity by explaining to it the economic forces against which it is struggling. These efforts are in a sense educational, as they try by appeals to reason to relate in the minds of the workers such variables as volume of production and standards of living; as, for example, by showing how much Danish bacon can be got for a ton of British coal. Perhaps the line between education in this sense and propaganda is finely drawn; personally I should not describe as education appeals to which the worker could give no reply, or of which he could not ask questions. But whether the medium is education or propaganda it must necessarily be clouded with political doctrine; any attempt to increase the industrial efficiency of a worker by trying to convince him that his standard of living, and that what he can buy for his wages, depends upon what he himself produces, provides endless opportunity for political debate. It is already difficult enough for industry to get its productive job done without its activities being further delayed while its workers are encouraged to debate ultimate political philosophies. The miners might readily accept a statement that a ton of coal sent out brings so much bacon in return; they might, however, still need to be convinced that a fair share of the bacon finds its way to the miner's breakfast table once it has got into the country.

But it is not the business of productive industry to preach any particular interpretation of economic fact or need. There is ample opportunity for questions of this kind to be debated inside the recognized political machinery: it is the business of the Government of the day to explain to the country what its economic policies are, and to submit them for constitutional approval. It cannot be an aim of education in industry to justify international rates of exchange or economic co-opera-tion in Europe. This, at the moment, is particularly true of nationalized industries.

But it is of cardinal importance that, once economic policies involving industrial planning have been decided upon, every single person in industry should understand what are the industrial implications of those policies. Every manager, fore-man, and worker should know clearly what the concern he is working for is trying to do and why it is trying to do it in the particular way that it has chosen; he should understand the difficulties of finance, manpower, supplies, and so forth with which his organization is faced, and he should be given as clear a picture as possible of where the organization is believed by its directors to be going. To describe this as education let us take a term from the *Report of the Trade Union Congress* held at Bridlington in 1949, and call it with them 'Industrial Educa-tion'. This is what they have to say.

Training and education should not be exclusively technical, but should attempt to infuse into officials and workpeople an enthusiasm for the success of the nationalised industry, with an explanation of its social and economic background and problems. Note has been taken of what is already being done in certain cases, but the General Council are of the opinion that there is need for a great expansion of effort on these lines.

It follows also that training of this character—or industrial education as it may be called—should be provided for both officials and for workpeople. Since many of the former have a long pre-nationalisation experience with its very different traditions it is particularly necessary that they should acquire a sincere desire to consult, in the fullest sense of the term, with workpeople's representatives.

Not everyone will be convinced that the expression 'Industrial Education' has any meaning. But there is clear enough agreement of the effects it ought to produce. Indeed, there are many effects that we could imagine produced and yet that we are quite unable to do anything whatever about: we cannot, for example, trisect an angle, though we can clearly see what we want to do. There is likewise no certainty that we can engender these economic faiths by educational means.

But many interesting educational experiments are being made to find out what we can do. In the nationalized industries the process of joint consultation has been made compulsory. This process, which consists in management, foremen, and workers freely discussing the operations of the industry so as to increase productivity or to reduce costs, is of some antiquity, and has been developed, if only superficially, into one of the working techniques of private enterprise, particularly in America. In the British mining industry every colliery has its consultative committee, and every area and division its council; there is a National Consultative Council for the industry as a whole. This hierarchy of councils and committees, over a thousand in all, are teaching themselves to discuss the mining operations, present and future, in which they are all engaged, their costs and efficiency, their scope and limitations, their incidental working problems of supply, distribution, and so forth; they discuss, too, the safety, health, and welfare of the mineworkers as well as the education and training of future officials and engineering staffs. We cannot pretend that consultation will solve any moral crisis, if that is the true difficulty in which Britain finds itself to-day; men sitting round a table talking about the proper way to solve the technical problems of their industry, while they may deal with their anti-social comrades, the absentees, and the saboteurs, can hardly be expected to change their whole scale of values as a result; something deeper is needed to convince ordinary men that society will work only so long as its members are prepared to put more into it than they expect to get out of it. But the first essential to the working of a technical society is co-opera-tion, and men co-operate only by agreement. Industrial demo-cracy demands agreement, and the best educational medium for ensuring this is consultation. It is only by wrestling with the living difficulties that men will see the otherwise invisible problems of their work, and there is more hope of them co-operating if they know the demon they are all supposed to be fighting. Nor is this all. Consultation not only should instruct both management and worker in how to tackle their common enemy; it should, by their alliance, help to remove the tradi-tional mistrust, the attitude towards authority that in the Army finds expression in the impersonal 'They'. But as the *T.U.C. Report* implies, it is of no use to approach consultation disin-genuously; it is no medium for half truth; and unless it is used with complete sincerity it had better not be used at all; the battle had better be fought in another arena. I can only say that in my view, consultation, as a form of industrial education, can do more than any single factor to improve industrial relations. Whether it will succeed in improving them to the extent that the country needs to get it out of its present economic toils, no one can predict. There certainly does not seem a great deal of time left for us to find other solutions; whether we shall be capable of agreeing among ourselves none of us can yet say. I do not think we shall be kept waiting long for the answer.

3

Educational Reorganization in Relation to the Social Order

I. L. KANDEL

In a period of social, political, and economic changes, when the full effects upon the culture of a group are not yet fully understood, the problems of education—its organization, aims, and content—increase and demand persistent attention. It is this situation that has aroused such widespread interest in the future of education not only in Great Britain but also in the United States and in other countries of the world. The educational planning which began in the early years of the war does not represent a new interest in education but is part of the whole programme of social reconstruction made imperative by a great variety of conditions. These conditions were themselves slow in developing but they had already begun to unfold gradually long before it was realized that they portended changes in education. The conditions were the results of the slow and gradual break with earlier traditions produced by the scientific development, by technological advances, by political and economic changes, by transfer of political power, and by changes in culture. For, despite the difficulty which some find in defining culture, the changes in it became increasingly obvious.

And yet, while the cultural changes which have taken place since the opening of the present century have been radical, something of the past continues to be carried along in them. The past is not only prologue; it gives meaning to the play as it unfolds. Even in those revolutions that claim to make a complete break with the past, its contributions and influence on the present cannot be ignored. This is not merely a form of cultural nostalgia, but a realization that a people's culture represents its customs, habits, ideas, ideals, and beliefs which have held it together and which it regards as valuable for its survival and perpetuation. Culture is like a nation, which Ernest Barker once defined as 'a house of thought which men have made that their minds may dwell there together'. This definition does not, however, deny the possibility of selection, modification, adaptation, and reinterpretation of that culture to meet new demands.

We are living in one of those periods when in education as in all aspects of life we stand on the threshold of a new era. The great moments in the history of education have always been those in which adjustments and adaptations have had to be made to the new demands of a changing culture, whether in its narrower or in its broader sense. This has always involved a consideration of the relations of the individual to society or the State, and of the kind of individual that society or the State wished to produce through the schools. But here it must be noted that the school is not the only agency of education. The tendency, however, is for the school to become charged with responsibilities previously discharged by other organizations.

It is significant that in those régimes in which the individual is regarded as a malleable tool of the State, no distinction is made between formal and informal education. In democracies, however, whose existence depends upon the co-operation and interest of intelligent citizens, the gradual decline of voluntary agencies in education can only be considered as a serious diminution of those competing forces which prevent the consolidation of authority in the hands of one central agency, whether, as Mill said in his famous discussion of State education, 'this be a monarch, or priesthood, an aristocracy, or a majority of the existing generation', and he might have added the political party in power.

Whatever adjustments must be made in education to meet the demands of cultural changes, its primary function has always remained the same through the ages. That function has always been to induct the young into the culture of the community, society, or nation of which they are to be members. As defined by Professor W. E. Hocking of Harvard University, the first function of education has at all times been to provide for the reproduction of the type, or, in other words, to promote and ensure the solidarity, preservation, and survival of the group. This reproduction of the type on the part of the adult members of a society flows from a desire for self-preservation and security, and on the part of the immature from a desire for acceptance or belongingness as members of the group. Hence conformism, or acculturation, or acceptance of a common language of discourse and common objects of allegiance is a natural process whereby the young are informally educated into membership in their group. Long before schools were established the young, not only in primitive but in Greek and Roman societies, learned the ways of their elders by a sort of apprenticeship or by imitation. Education was an unconscious process of socialization. And long before school existed each family in each occupation assumed the responsibility of training up the child or youth in the way he should go. When schools were established for the purpose of providing formal education, their task was to impart those aspects of a society's culture—its skills, its traditions, its ideas, and its beliefs—which were considered to be most vital or important for its stability, perpetuation, and unity.

This function—the conservation or transmission of the cultural or social heritage—is still the primary object of education and is intended to equip the younger generation with the skills and knowledge and ideals which will enable it to take its place in the social group and contribute to its survival. There is also another purpose, which is to provide the future members of a society with a common language of discourse, common understanding, and common objects of allegiance on the basis of which they may be able to co-operate for their mutual welfare and the welfare of society.

Two issues immediately arise. The first is who shall determine the content of the common education, and the second is whether all children and youth should be educated in the same schools. Both issues were discussed by John Stuart Mill in the well-known passage in his *Essay on Liberty*. Time has shown, however, that it is possible to have a publicly maintained system of education in which the content of education is not dictated or prescribed officially, but is developed by those directly responsible for its transmission—by the teachers on the basis of their professional preparation, through official suggestions, and through guidance from inspectors. At the same time the dangers that Mill foresaw have been proved to be real in the educational systems of totalitarian régimes which have been deliberately designed to establish a despotism over the mind.

Fear of that despotism over the mind through action of a central authority has become fear of its exercise in the classroom, a fear which manifests itself in the opposition to imposition or indoctrination. There is here a failure to realize that if certain values, whether intellectual or moral, are desirable either for the welfare of society or for the development of the individual, the pupils must be indoctrinated in them not unintelligently, not by rote learning, not by coercion, but with full understanding of their meanings.

The second issue—whether all children and youth should be educated in the same school—is one that has only recently begun to be discussed. It arose first as a protest against the traditional organization of education into dual systems—one for the masses and the other for the well-to-do, the one free and the other charging fees, the one provided by the public authorities and the other to a certain degree private. From the point of view of public policy the argument put forward against the dual system is that, educated in separate schools, the members of different social strata do not learn to understand each other, and the system helps to perpetuate a social cleavage between the upper and lower classes which Disraeli described as 'two nations'.

Another cause of the protest against the continued existence of the dual system is based on the fact that fee-paying private schools have a different curriculum from that of the public primary schools and further help to perpetuate the differences between the social classes by serving directly as schools preparatory to the secondary schools. The result is that those who already enjoy certain advantages, particularly small classes, have the additional advantage in the competition for admission to the secondary schools.

The objections to the continued existence of the dual system of schools and a desire to give all future citizens a common foundation and a common language of discourse and to equalize educational opportunities inspired the movement in France for *l'école unique* and in Weimar Germany for the *Einheitsschule* —the idea of the common school. In Germany the movement succeeded in securing the abolition, by a provision in the Weimar Constitution, of the *Vorschule* or the school preparatory to the secondary school, and the substitution therefor of the four-year *Grundschule*. In France the change was less drastic— the free-charging *classes préparatoires* were not abolished but their specialized curriculum and teachers were replaced by the curriculum prescribed for the public elementary schools and by teachers certificated as elementary-school teachers.

The United States is, of course, the home of the common school which is attended by almost all the children of all the people; the majority of the 10 per cent. of the pupils not in public schools attend denominational, mainly Roman Catholic, schools. The American public school has undoubtedly played an important part in Americanizing the younger generations drawn from so many different strains of nationality, race, and creeds. Nevertheless, the homogeneity that has been produced has been somewhat superficial and has not prevented the emergence of conflicts and tensions found in other countries which have not had common school systems.

The difficulty of securing complete homogeneity in a country as large and as diversified as the United States is great. Nor can the school be held responsible for those tensions that emerge from economic and other conditions. Nevertheless, despite the existence of common schools, one of the serious problems with which they are at present confronted is to develop and promote a programme of inter-cultural education whose aim would be to educate the pupils of different national, racial, and religious backgrounds to respect each other and work together. Nor, on the other hand, does the fact that children of all classes attend the same school *eliminate* consciousness of class distinctions or equalize all conditions as some recent investigations in the United States have shown. This is not a condemnation of the American public school, but rather evidence that the school cannot change but reflects the social structure.

Whether all pupils should be required to attend the same school, at any rate for their elementary education, was an issue discussed in the days of the Weimar Republic. The question then debated was whether the principle of compulsory education implied that all children must be educated, leaving the choice of school to their parents, or that they must all attend the same school. In other words, the question was whether *Erziehungszwang* meant *Schulzwang*. An attempt made by the legislature of the State of Oregon to compel all children to attend public schools—a plan aimed at private denominational schools—was declared unconstitutional in 1926.

There seems to be a general assumption on the part of those who support the idea of educating all children in one school that this is the way to secure homogeneity of beliefs, ideas, ideals, and so on—all those aspects of a culture that appear to be essential for social cohesion. This is, of course, the totalitarian concept of culture and of education within that culture. Democratic educators would at once disavow this concept, and yet in their eagerness to guarantee equality of educational opportunities to all children, irrespective of accident of residence and of family circumstances, some would advocate the common school rather than common education for all up to a certain point.

Up to the present the existence of private schools at the primary level does not appear to have been an object of serious attack in England. The suggestion has been made that those found inefficient and defective should be closed—a suggestion which the Ministry of Education has been empowered to carry out under the provisions of the Education Act, 1944. Parents may have the right to choose the type of school that they wish for their children, but the State or society in its own interests has the duty of seeing to it that private or independent schools provide instruction and education which are at least as good as in the publicly maintained schools.

It is somewhat paradoxical that, while some educational reformers are ready to substitute the multilateral school for different types of secondary schools, they have not proposed the creation of a system of common primary schools for all. And yet the foundations for common attitudes, common loyalties, and common understanding between future citizens are laid in the primary school. Here a common curriculum that would equip the pupils with the necessary skills and knowledge for future studies is essential; the methods of instruction may vary according to the abilities of the pupils. At the secondary-school level, however, while certain subjects must be studied by all pupils, the curricula must be differentiated in accordance with their abilities and interests. This is, in fact, the system of Scandinavia where the differentiation of secondary schools does not appear adversely to affect social homogeneity. It may indeed be true that the common primary school has, as the Scandinavians claim, established in the course of more than a century of compulsory education the basic ideas of national classlessness.

Not enough thought has, in fact, been given to the problem of the kinds of education that would have to be provided to adapt it to the ages, abilities, and aptitudes of the pupils. The dominant ideas are that equality of educational opportunities can best be assured and sympathetic understanding between different social classes be promoted by putting all pupils into the same secondary school.

A great deal is made of the assumption that the ability and aptitude of a child cannot be discovered at the age of eleven or twelve. In the context in which the three A's (age, ability, and aptitude) appear, it is clear that the reference is to studies appropriate at the secondary-school level. With reference to what have been the traditional characteristics of a secondary-school curriculum—languages and mathematics—President James B. Conant of Harvard University has stated in his recent book, *Education in a Divided World*, that 'There is considerable evidence to indicate that linguistic and mathematical ability can be recognized in the early high school years'. President Conant seems to deplore the fact that the American comprehensive high school—the multilateral secondary school —provides so little opportunity for those who have ability in languages and mathematics. Provision is made for those who have musical or artistic talent, 'but relatively little is done for those who have comparable talent in languages and mathematics. Yet how much society has to gain by the early recognition of such people and their adequate education!'

Dr. Conant clearly states the dilemma that has faced American educators for some time and that must be faced by English educators. The problem is to define the meaning of equality of educational opportunity in such a way that all pupils receive the same general instruction by virtue of the fact that they will all have the same rights and duties and also that education which is best adapted to their abilities. Since the primary function of education is to provide for reproduction of the type, there must be a certain unity or common foundation in the programme of education. There is, however, a second function which is defined by Hocking as education for growth beyond the type, that is, education for the fullest development of each individual in accordance with his abilities and interests. As pupils mature, account must increasingly be taken of their individual differences of ability and appropriate instruction be provided for them.

To admit the existence of individual differences of ability, which the advocates of the multilateral school have not yet denied, inevitably means the acceptance of the idea of selection and distribution. The methods so far adopted may not have reached perfection but they have not been proved to be entirely futile. Only those who refuse to face the real meaning of democracy will regard selection and distribution based on adequate methods as a threat to that equality of opportunity which they are so anxious to establish. National interest requires first that there be a body of citizens as highly educated as the ability of each individual permits, and, secondly, that opportunities be provided for the discovery and training of those who show the ability to profit by that training, and to make their contributions in the various fields of the nation's complex activities.

Why, it will be asked, cannot these ends be achieved in one and the same school which caters for pupils of all types of abilities, and at the same time does not run the risk of intensifying social differences or of perpetuating a class system of education? President Conant, in the book already cited, states the problem and virtually admits the failure of the system that he considers to be irreplaceable. In one passage he writes:

> We could not, if we would, separate into different school buildings those who wish to enter the professions *via* the universities and all others. Except in certain cities, our high school pupils come together in one school which serves the community. Such differentiation as is required will be within one school and should be so arranged as to create as little social distinction as possible.

But apparently the system does not work as ideally as Dr. Conant would like to see it work, because, as he frequently admits, the able pupils are neglected; he writes:

> I wish some organization identified in the public mind with concern for *all* American youth would take some democratic action to demonstrate a vigorous interest in the gifted boy or girl. This would serve as an encouragement to all teachers. The schools should be stimulated in a direction which in some quarters has been rather spurned as being undemocratic and old-fashioned. A National Commission for the Identification of Talented Youth has been suggested by one group of educators.

It is clear from the context and from other statements in Dr. Conant's book that, whatever the strong points of the American comprehensive high school may be, they have failed to provide for the education of the intellectually able pupils.

When the comprehensive high school began to replace the separate types of schools, it was expected that the academic curriculum would be retained intact as new curricula were added to meet the widening range of individual differences of ability among all the pupils attending the school. That expectation has not been fulfilled. The separate and distinct curricula were gradually replaced by a long list of subjects, some required, some elective. Inevitably a teacher, confronted with a class of pupils of heterogeneous abilities, was compelled to cater for the average. As described in the report, *General Education in a Free Society*, prepared by a Harvard University Committee, the result was a system which was 'too fast for the slow and too slow for the fast', and marked by 'a colorless mean'. Since able students likely to profit from an academic or grammar-school course constitute a minority, estimated by Dr. Conant at 30 per cent., the tendency has set in to depreciate the academic course and to substitute for it 'common learnings', work experience, and vocational training in the education of *all* American youth.

But it is not only the able pupils who fail to receive the attention that they deserve. Two years ago the former United States Commissioner of Education appointed a committee to recommend what should be done for about three million boys and girls, presumably below average, who were deriving little profit from their stay in high school.

In the light of these facts it would have been interesting if Dr. Conant had defined what he meant by the 'undemocratic and old-fashioned' direction that he hoped would result from the recommendations of his proposed National Commission for Identification of Talent. I believe that it would point to the organization of a variety of types of schools, each with its own definite aims and curricula, but each in its own way contributing to the main aim, common to all, of producing young men and women educated in accordance with their abilities as future citizens and human beings with broad interests and with some clear idea of a purpose in life.

It will, however, be objected that the separation of pupils

in different schools will perpetuate social cleavages and prevent the development of mutual understanding and of democratic ideals. Again American experience may be drawn upon. The comprehensive high school is the common school for all children of all the people. One of the fundamental arguments adduced in its favour is that the common school breaks down class barriers and class distinctions. How far this is from the facts may be gathered from a study of this particular question in the book, *Who Shall Be Educated?* by Warner, Havighurst, and Loeb. The authors found that social class distinctions not only determine the organization of pupils' clubs and leadership, but also the choice of courses.

Since that book appeared, the statement on the effect of social class status on the choice of studies has been confirmed in *Elmtown's Youth*, a sociological survey of a mid-western town by A. B. Hollingshead of Yale University. 'The high school curriculum', he writes, 'is organized around three courses: college preparatory, general, and commercial. Enrolment in each course is related very significantly to class position; that is, each course acts either to attract or repel students in the different prestige classes.' The fact, stated in the earlier book, that social class differences are not broken down because the children of all social levels attend the same school, is also confirmed in the later book. It must be recalled that one of the strongest arguments for the common school in the United States is that it would help to develop common bonds between the pupils drawn from a great variety of heterogeneous social and cultural backgrounds. The evidence so far available does not point to success. This does not mean that the school has failed, but that the school cannot eliminate prejudice acquired by the pupils in their environment outside the school. More evidence of the same kind can be found in W. Lloyd Warner's *Democracy in Jonesville*.

The example of the United States cannot be ignored. That there is an awareness there of the weaknesses of the high school is apparent from the literature cited and from a great many other studies that cannot be quoted here. Nevertheless, the

United States was the first nation in the world to undertake the experiment of providing equality of educational opportunity for all. The lessons to be learned from the American comprehensive high school are that individual differences of ability cannot be ignored, that different types of education best adapted to these differences cannot be successfully offered in the same school without sacrificing standards and values, and that mere juxtaposition of pupils in the same school or even in the same classroom does not produce mutual understanding and respect between different social classes.

In the very laudable desire to create a system of education which would provide equality of educational opportunities, there has been too widespread a tendency to devote attention to organization and to ignore the problems of curricula and methods and content of instruction. From the arguments in favour of the multilateral school it would appear as though all that is necessary is to put the three types of schools—grammar, modern, and technical—together in one school, even before any careful thought has been given to the kind of curricula that would be offered in the modern and technical schools. It seems to be assumed that the mere creation of the multilateral school would solve the problems of allocation of pupils, of curricula and teachers, and of social attitudes.

There is no reason to suppose that the problem of allocating pupils to the courses best suited to their abilities would be easier after they have entered a school than before entrance. The same measures of competence would have to be used—primary school records, examinations, tests of intelligence and achievement, and so on. Nor is there any evidence that pupils or parents would be any happier about allocation to one course rather than another in the same school than they are reported to be about allocation to one school rather than another. Too much is made of the technical difficulties of transferring pupils from one school to another more appropriate to them. And, finally, there is a tendency to abuse the term 'democratic'. The provision of equality of educational opportunities is democratic, but to go farther and assume that to have all pupils in the same school is more democratic than to allocate them to different schools according to their abilities is an assumption that is not borne out by American practice, nor is it in accord with all that is known about individual differences of ability.

The problem of organizing an educational system in which the right pupils will receive the right education from the right teacher under conditions by which they can best profit from it is not simple. The definition itself is not new, for it is a statement of the function of educational administration as defined in a lecture delivered in Oxford some thirty years ago by the late Sir Graham Balfour. The problem is not simple, nor is it to be solved by the simple device of putting all pupils indiscriminately into the same school. The English tradition, it is claimed, will prevent making the same mistakes that have produced the defects of the American comprehensive high school. It is difficult to know what English tradition will be followed as a guide in a completely new venture. It is forgotten that only forty years ago it was expected in the United States that one tradition—the academic—would be able to withstand the attacks made upon it in the interests of 'democratic' education. Perhaps after all in this period of reorganization the direction to follow is that implicit in Dr. Conant's statement— one which is no less democratic even though spurned by some as 'undemocratic and old-fashioned'.

4

Intellectual Freedom and the Schools

J. F. WOLFENDEN

EDUCATION is essentially the influence of one person on another. Alcibiades' father sent him to learn wisdom from Socrates just as in our own day a man of substance might send his son to Henry Cotton to be taught golf. The individual with a reputation, in whatever field, influences other individuals, and teaches them, by whatever technique he may adopt, what he already knows himself. He may be a sophist of Hellas; she may be Lady Elizabeth Hastings, of whom it was said that 'to love her was a liberal education'; it may even be a tutorial in this University, where one scholar, young or old, smokes at another. Always the influence is that of one mind, one personality, one character on another. That, at any rate, is how it all begins.

But Socrates had other pupils besides Alcibiades. And it is not long before a school comes into existence. It is often said that the family is the first school a child attends, and in a metaphorical sense that may be allowed. But it is only in a metaphorical (and rather misleading) sense that it is true. For in a family there is no free choice of instructor—or, indeed, of pupils. And whatever else a family may or may not be, it is hard to maintain that it is a community brought into existence for the sake of education; whereas that is exactly what a school is.

It might seem that Socrates or Gorgias or Protagoras enjoyed the fullest possible intellectual freedom. They knew no inspectors, their pupils sat for no external examinations, employers in Attica demanded no certificates of education, particular or general. Not even at Sparta, where there was a highly developed system of universal free elementary education, was there any signs of the doctrine that public money involves public control. And yet, although these formal constraints were unknown, there was in fact one almighty and inescapable controlling force. It might be called public opinion. But in crude and brutal language it amounted to this, that the fathers who paid the piper called the tune. It is almost incredible, until it is calmly observed, that in Athens, the most civilized, tolerant, intellectually awake society the Western world has ever known—or so we are constantly told—the most distinguished headmaster of the century was not translated to a bishop's palace or the mastership of a Cambridge college, but, after public trial, judicially executed. It is hard to realize that that was how the Hellenic spirit of free inquiry manifested itself. And it is harder still to remember that that was the limit —and a pretty stern one—to intellectual freedom in ancient Greece. The principle is a simple one, that a man who sets up in business has to please his customers; and it makes no difference whether what he sells is wisdom or bathing costumes. That principle, as a matter of fact, applies to independent schools to-day; and if the dissatisfaction of parents is less strikingly expressed nowadays than it was in Athens in the fourth century B.C., that may simply be because the education of their children is less important to them than it was to the fathers of Plato and Pheidippides. We shall do well not to forget the influence on education of those who pay for it, whether as individuals deliberately choosing one school rather than another or as anonymous tax-payers and rate-payers who are ultimately responsible for all that is done on their behalf by administrators, national or local.

Our purpose is not to give an historical summary of education from the time of the Sophists down to the present day. Let us jump more than 2,000 years and more than 1,200 miles, with two comments only. First, it must be remembered that from the date of the establishment of Christianity onwards, education in this country was in the hands of the Church. And that must have meant that in theory at any rate the expression of opinion was rather narrowly circumscribed. Innovators in other fields, geography or natural science for instance, soon found that they had a plain choice between recantation and decapitation; and it cannot be maintained, with the best will in the world, that intellectual freedom was a characteristic of the educational activities of the Christian Church. The Reformation, incidentally, brought no relief in this respect; there are other intolerances besides that of the Roman Church. Secondly, we must note the 'free' grammar schools of the fifteenth and following centuries. They seem to have developed 'out of schools attached to places of religion. Gradually they moved away, in curriculum, from the traditional subjects of instruction, which had been as strictly 'vocational' in their day as anything we know in ours. In what precise sense they were 'free' has been much debated (not least in the columns of the *Oxford English Dictionary* and in the footnotes of the Fleming Report), but two meanings of the adjective seem to attach to them indisputably, that they provided an education without cost and that they eventually achieved freedom from outside authority, ecclesiastical or political. They are the lineal ancestors of the independent schools of to-day. The only sad thing is that many of them, though they survive to this day, are no longer free in the functional sense, though they now are in the merely financial sense. It is a wry commentary that their real freedom has been swallowed up in costlessness.

We must skip rapidly through the nineteenth century, sketching in only very roughly the main features of the educational landscape. First there were the independent schools, anciently established, recovering slowly from their disgraceful eighteenth-century torpor, and, with the advent of a new moneyed class, widely imitated. In each of these the reputation of the school rose or declined with a particular headmaster. For it was true of them as of the schools of Hellas that the individual was the educator. Parents sent their sons to Butler or to Arnold or to Thring, as they later sent them to Sanderson, not primarily because they wanted particular subjects or particular games or even a particular tie, but because they wanted the influence and ideals of a particular man. And to the extent to which such a man commanded the respect of the relevant public, to that extent his school flourished.

The second obvious feature of the nineteenth century is the gradual awakening of the public conscience to the illiteracy (in the strict sense of the word) of those whose parents could not afford the only kind of education which had hitherto been available. The stages of that awakening are well known. Here almost at once arose those religious, or, more strictly, sectarian, differences whose embers have burst into uncomfortable flame right down to 1944. In the Nonconformist strongholds of the north there are alive to-day many who have fought and suffered for their right to an education free from the formularies of the Established Church. And there is a tangled and violent history of disputes about the propriety or impropriety of using public money for schools where distinctive doctrine was taught. We begin to see here a gradual and probably unconscious shift of emphasis, for now for the first time the State, through the public purse, becomes a real power in educational affairs. From that day to this its influence has grown, until at the present time public money, either from taxes or from rates, governs to a much greater extent than any ecclesiastical authority the pattern of the education of the country. The first education grant was made (almost by accident) in 1833 to the National Society and the British and Foreign School Society. The Acts of 1870, 1899, and 1902 laid the foundations, and pretty solid ones they have turned out to be, of the system of public education we know to-day. On them has been built the present-day edifice of primary, secondary, and further education, with its almost innumerable accompaniments of school meals, school medical service, nursery schools, youth service, village colleges, its teachers' training colleges, education committees, attendance officers, and directors of education.

Now we have reached, rather breathlessly, the present day. We look round at this variegated pattern and we ask: 'What of intellectual freedom in the schools?' And that question immediately arouses another: 'Freedom from what?' or, more positively, 'Freedom for what?'

The clear answer to that is implicit in the first sentence of this lecture. If education is in essence the influence of one person on another, then the freedom we are discussing is the freedom of the teacher to exercise that influence and of the pupil to receive it. Furthermore, that freedom ought to be granted at all stages and levels of the educational hierarchy. At the university level it is not seriously questioned, at any rate westwards of the Iron Curtain. It is accepted that within broad and generous limits a university is an autonomous body; and very few professors or college tutors can be conscious of any encroachment from outside on the intellectual freedom they have a right to enjoy. But with the schools it is otherwise. A variety of influences has produced a situation to which head-masters react, according to their temperament, with exasperation, bitterness, or despair, and which, at the very least, calls for serious and thorough investigation.

Let us look, very briefly, at some of these influences. First and foremost there remains in continuous activity that force which killed Socrates, the influence of the man who pays the piper. In those schools which still charge fees, by now a very small proportion of the whole, this influence is exercised directly, as a father chooses one school rather than another for his son's education. But for the schools inside the national system, where this direct fee-paying operation does not occur, the influence is exerted indirectly, either by or on behalf of the people's elected representatives sitting in parliament or on local education authorities. It is exerted by them when they make laws or pass resolutions in an education committee. It is exerted on their behalf when administrators, national or local, harness their considerable abilities to the job of carrying out the decisions of their masters.

Now I do not want to be misunderstood. I do not suggest that my friends in the Ministry of Education and in the offices of the local education authorities spend their days and nights deliberately designing ways of limiting the liberty of those who live and work in the schools. But as a matter of practical fact that is what happens, very largely by accident and very slightly

by design. At the university level, as I have said, interference
from outside does not occur. But what would a college tutor
say if he were told, from outside the university altogether, that
his pupils might not take their Schools until they had reached
an arbitrarily fixed age by an arbitrarily fixed date? What
would the governing body of a college say if it were told that
although officially recognized by the Ministry of Education as
efficient, it was nevertheless subject to inspection by officials
of a local authority (not a local education authority) carrying
out duties imposed by another ministry altogether? What
would the senior tutor of a college say if he were required to
keep a register of his undergraduates and record their atten-
dances at morning and afternoon sessions? These are not fantastic fictions. Each of these infringements of normal freedom
is in operation at this moment, and, what is more, each of
them applies to the schools charmingly labelled 'independent'.
They, in turn, are free from a mass of restrictions which affect
other types of school.

There is time for no more than these few examples; but I think
they are significant. The trouble springs from two roots, from
ignorance, on the part of legislators, of the real function of
teachers and schools, and from zealous tidy-mindedness on the
part of administrators. And there is developing, incidentally,
a divergence of interest between the administrators and the
people, whom, officially, they serve. Now that children are
sorted out, at the age of eleven, and directed into one of three
main streams of secondary education, there is increasing bitterness and disillusion on the part of the general public; they had
not understood that 'secondary education for all' meant that
their own children would be branded at the age of eleven, by
what seems to them a heartlessly impersonal 'education office',
as unfit for a grammar-school education. To the increasing
power of the administrator we shall have to return; meanwhile,
let it be clear that this increase in his influence is not wholly his
fault—it is part of the general trend of the times towards in-
venting an expert and then giving him control.

The second major controlling influence is that of the external examination. I am not going to plead that all external examinations should be abolished; I am not at all convinced that it would be a good thing if they were. But I do say that to the extent to which the content of the education we provide in our schools is determined by the requirements of external examinations, to that extent we are less than free in deciding what we shall teach and how we shall teach it. Whether that is a good thing or not, it is a plain fact.

I wish I could feel more confident than I do that the current changes in the certificate examinations will help the schools in this respect. So far as I can see, there are at least three dangers which will arise from the new arrangements. The first is that whereas the much-maligned old School Certificate was a rough-and-ready yard-stick adopted by many of the professions and a wide variety of employers, there is no guarantee that we shall not in future be driven to taking in the schools the first examinations of a host of different professions, each with its own peculiar syllabus. Secondly, with an arbitrary age-limit imposed on the examination structure, we shall find ourselves controlled by the examination syllabus for two consecutive years in each relevant form, since in each summer term some members of a form will, and some will not, be of an age to take an examination for which all are equally fit and ready. There is no escape from this except the retrograde device of arranging forms by age instead of by ability and attainment. If ever there was a naked external intervention in the internal arrangements of a school this is it. Thirdly, and most serious of all, there is clear evidence that the examination tail is wagging the teaching dog. That comes about in this way. One or two of the examining bodies now have so many candidates that they have to have an army of examiners in each subject. If the markings of these different fallible human beings are to be kept in line with each other, the questions must be set in such a way as to permit the smallest possible range of subjective difference in marking between one examiner and another. If questions are set in this way teachers will teach for them in this way; and so not only the subject-matter but the approach and method of teaching will be to a large extent determined by the sheer bulk of the number of examinees. Add to this that in at any rate one of the examining bodies the number of candidates who are deemed to have passed or to have deserved a 'Credit' is a fixed percentage of the total number of candidates for each subject, and you reach the entertaining conclusion that the schools could of their own motion depress the standard of a Pass or a Credit by putting in for the examination a large number of candidates who were known to be incapable of passing it. That measure of freedom, if they care to exercise it, they do enjoy.

I am not sure that the universities are fully awake to their responsibilities in this matter of external examinations. For so long as there are open scholarship papers of the existing type, in whatever faculty, for so long we in the schools must inevitably teach our sixth forms on the lines which the scholarship papers require. And the same is true of Science Prelims. here and First M.B. or the Mechanical Sciences Qualifying Examination elsewhere. It is our job—or so the piper-paying parent firmly asserts—to get our boys through these examinations, if their passing one of them is a necessary condition of their following a career in medicine, engineering, or whatever it may be. And it therefore follows that the universities, either by their statutory requirements for entry or through college examinations, determine almost entirely the work of the sixth forms of the schools which feed them. I am not saying that this is a bad thing. But I am saying that it is a fact, and that the universities have the greater part of the responsibility for the content and method of our sixth-form teaching. That is why we in the schools are sometimes rather indignant when the universities blame us for what they call our over-specialization, whereas the plain fact is that the degree of specialization we practise is imposed on us by college scholarship examinations and university faculty requirements. And that is why I have heard a headmaster say that he no longer has any voice in the curriculum of the upper part of his school; all he does is to 'lay on' what each boy wants for some external examination at the university or in his intended profession.

But I believe that there is an illness more deep-seated and serious than any of these. To some extent these limitations of freedom have caused it; to some extent it is the fault of the teaching profession itself. Let me tell you a true story to illustrate what I mean. In a county borough north of the Trent the Education Committee was discussing the proper rate of pay for some teachers who had been engaged in some work of supervision on a Saturday evening. The Chairman turned to one of his colleagues and said: 'Can Alderman *X* tell us what they do in his Committee about bus-drivers who work extra shifts?' Alderman *X* informed the Education Committee that bus-drivers employed by the Corporation are paid time-and-a-half for extra shifts. 'Right,' says the Chairman of the Education Committee, 'then we'll give the teachers time-and-a-half; I reckon that what is proper for bus-drivers is right enough for teachers.' Now I think the natural first reaction of anybody concerned with education is one of indignation that bus-drivers, excellent men as they are, should be taken as the canon or standard of reference for teachers; and with that indignation I should sympathize. But it goes a stage deeper than that. The sad part of the story is that the teaching profession as a whole should enjoy a public reputation which invites such a comparison. And I think that that arises from many causes, from a general decline of public respect for learning, from an excessive control by administrators of what goes on inside a school, from what I hope I may be forgiven for calling a trade union attitude on the part of many teachers themselves, all adding up to a general feeling of defeatism and lack of self-respect. It is all of a piece with the regulation, only recently revoked after considerable to-do from teachers, that in order to take a party of children to a gas-works or a coal-mine or a cathedral during school hours application had to be made to the office of the local authority, countersigned by His Majesty's Inspector, for each separate and several visit. It is not easy to build up, or even to maintain, self-respect in a profession which has to ask for such permission in such a way for such a purpose.

Especially this creeping paralysis of defeatism is felt in the grammar schools. The grammar schools feel, rightly or wrongly, that they are getting a raw deal. Everywhere they look, and on every issue that crops up, they seem to lose. In salary negotiations they are outvoted by the sheer number of teachers in other kinds of school. The consequence of that is an inadequate allowance for university degrees and a comparative depression of their value. And that in its turn makes it yet more difficult to get good men to come to the grammar schools instead of going to industry and research. In the name of democracy the three recognized types of secondary school must be accepted as equal in status and reputation. The consequence of that is that the traditions of academic learning inherited and transmitted by the grammar schools are discredited (even by spokesmen of the Ministry of Education) and jettisoned for the sake of an artificial 'parity of esteem' which is based neither on popular demand nor on educational fact. The growth of administrative power hits particularly those schools which have in the past enjoyed a form of independence comparable with what has been customary in the independent schools technically so called. The consequence of that is that grammar schoolmasters, and especially grammar school headmasters, are beginning to feel that they are no longer trusted to run their own show as they have been accustomed to do. It is now a principle accepted by more than one local education authority that not just the Chief Education Officer and his deputy but also the heads of departments must be paid more than headmasters because they control (that is the operative word) the schools and therefore the headmasters.

For all these reasons there is a drift away from the grammar schools. The headmasters feel that their job is no longer what it was; either they are looking over their shoulders at the education office or they are rather cynically finding 'ways round'. In either case they lose their self-respect and their integrity, personal and professional. They see comparatively junior members of their staffs, whom they could never conscientiously recommend for headmasterships, appointed to posts in the service of local education authorities and becoming the 'controllers' of headmasters. Or they see men whom they would label 'failed schoolmasters' moving into the inspectorate, national or local, and then inspecting and reporting on work which the reporters themselves have done with something less than unqualified success. Are these headmasters likely to be doing a full and vigorous job? Are they likely to be encouraging, either by example or by suggestion, able boys in their own schools to enter the teaching profession? Unfortunately, the whole process is a circle of the most vicious kind. The head-masters feel that they have a professional grievance. It is not simply, or even chiefly, a matter of salary—that is a symptom rather than a cause—it is a matter of the importance their job was once held to have and seems to have no longer. And because they feel like this, they become less and less able to do that job properly. And therefore the external checks grow more and more. And therefore fewer and fewer men of quality will come into the grammar schools. Unless this circle can be broken, the tradition of the grammar schools will go; and the chief sufferers from that will be not the schools themselves but the universities.

So far I have considered, naturally enough, the schools in the old grammar school tradition, whose links with the universities have been strong and ancient. Let us now think for a moment of a quite different type of school, the secondary modern school which came to birth in the Education Act of 1944. It is important that we should do so not only because this type of school caters for the bulk of the child population but also because the secondary modern school may well turn out to be this country's distinctive contribution to educational practice in this century—on one condition. We know well enough the criticisms the secondary modern school has had to face already —that new secondary modern is no more than old elementary writ large, that in neither buildings nor staff can it properly be called 'secondary', that the claim made for it, of parity with the grammar school of history, is baseless and indeed fantastic. But think for a minute of its opportunities, remote as they may be from university studies and standards. There is the opportunity here for a universal raising of the standard of the whole of the people, for sowing the seeds of what neither this country nor any other has so far enjoyed, an educated democracy. I am far from being one of those who decry—as is so fashionable to-day—intellectual ability and scholarly performance. But I do recognize, we all ought to respect, the gifts of that majority of the British people which is not academic in interest or capacity; and I am enough of a disciple of Edward Thring to demand that they should be given, like others, an education appropriate to their abilities and aptitudes. The possible consequences of this extended and properly designed education are incalculable—on one condition. That condition is that these schools should be free—free to develop their own techniques and their own excellences; free to manage their own affairs and to grow into self-respecting communities. I can see no reason in the nature of the universe why the secondary modern school in the back streets of an industrial town, with all its handicaps of Victorian barrack buildings, asphalt playgrounds and inadequate equipment, should have less right to be a free and self-governing community than the most wealthy and lovely college in this university. I am tempted to say that the consequences, for our democratic way of life, of a vigorous and powerful system of secondary modern schools will be greater than anything that could emerge from the universities, ancient or modern. Their initial handicaps are terrifying; they need—that is to say, seventy per cent. of our population needs—every possible help. And I suggest that what they need first and above all is the self-respect that can come only from freedom. Their headmasters must be as free as their colleagues in other forms of secondary school have been in the past: they must be deliberately led along the path of freedom by directors of education and education committees. If this can be established as their normal atmosphere, the battles of their colleagues will not have been in vain. It may turn out that this half-century, for one reason or another, will see the gradual decline of the grammar schools. That will be a grievous loss. But if during the same period the modern schools grow correspondingly in stature, and in consequence influence, it is not inconceivable that the ultimate balance will show a gain. There are signs already that enlightened education authorities are aware of their opportunity, and that to the modern schools are going men and women of a quality equal to that opportunity. Here is the beginning of a circle precisely opposite to the depressing and vicious circle in the grammar schools. It starts and ends in freedom.

So far my emphasis has been primarily on headmasters and only secondarily on schools. That seems to me to be only natural, since apart altogether from the occupational disease from which every headmaster suffers, of identifying his school with himself, these restraints and interferences inevitably hit the headmaster first and the school through him. He takes the knock and either absorbs it or transmits it to his colleagues and his pupils, that is, to his school.

It is not hard to see what are the effects inside a school of the influences we have been considering. It is axiomatic that a school is, or ought to be, a community. If it is to be that it must be able to breathe freely, to expand and grow in ways and directions appropriate to its own nature, in short, to live its own life. Ask any headmaster or headmistress how far this self-determining life is possible in present conditions. The answer will depend on two major factors. The first is the extent to which the headmaster or headmistress is personally capable of exercising the freedom which we all profess to desire. The second will be expressed in some such words as these—'It all depends on the particular local education authority'. The first of these factors we have already considered, and in our consideration we have found some grounds for disquiet. The second gives away the whole educational show in this country at the present time, and it must be further examined.

We who work in independent schools fail, sometimes, to recognize our good fortune. There are the constraints I have mentioned, from external examinations and from the parent who pays the piper. This latter is important, for the brutally simple reason that the financial solvency of an independent school, into which no public money flows, depends on the ability and willingness of a sufficient number of parents to pay the high fees which independence involves. One regrettable consequence of this is that some headmasters have to spend far too much of their time acting as salesmen; and another is that sometimes a headmaster is deterred from experiment or from following his own ideals and ambitions by doubts about his ability to carry parents with him in his projects. It may be, since not even headmasters are infallible, that this particular external check is salutary enough—provided that it stops short of what happened to Socrates. Nevertheless, it remains true that financial anxiety is seldom for long absent from the minds of those who are responsible for independent schools. On the other hand, each such school is in the hands of an independent body of Governors, the permanent trustees of the school's life: and in my own experience I must say that I have never, in fifteen years, had anything but wholly disinterested and wise support from such bodies. They take it as their function to hinder hindrances to the good life of the school, they do not concern themselves with its day-to-day management, and they do not try to do the headmaster's job—any more than he, if he is wise, will try to do theirs.

But the independent schools are a tiny fraction of the whole. I believe that they are important, and that their continued existence is important, because I believe it is important that there should continue to exist free institutions and free associations outside the control of the State—whether they are schools, universities, churches, trade unions, or lawn tennis clubs.

With the vast mass of schools the situation is far otherwise. It all depends, as I have said, on the particular local education authority. Some local education authorities are excellent, with a policy as enlightened as that of any independent governing body, and with far more resources in men, materials, and money than any one school could conceivably command. An administrator with ideals and vision, serving a local education authority with a sense of responsibility and plenty of money, has the most glorious opportunity the educational world has to offer at the present time. And there are some who seize this opportunity with both hands. Usually, they are humble men of heart, who openly say that their duty is to make administration the handmaid of the teachers—and that is good etymology, besides being good practice. The best of them—and this is not a merely circular definition of 'best'—are those who by their personalities and policies attract the best teachers and then give them the widest possible scope, the fullest possible freedom for the flow of the influence with which we began this lecture. Their view coincides with that of a great headmaster, now Bishop of Peterborough, when he says 'all whose duty is in administration should as far as possible stand out of the way for the teachers to do their appointed work, remembering that the purpose and *raison d'être* of all educational administration is to bring the right children before the right teachers at the right time and under the right conditions'.

But there are, it must be said, others, who hold a different view—or at any rate pursue a different practice. Often they suffer from excess of administrative zeal, so that machinery becomes an end in itself. Sometimes they display a passion for tidiness, so that their ideal is uniformity. Now and then they seem, and this is the most terrible thing, to be by temperament the enemies, instead of the friends and colleagues, of their teachers, and especially of their headmasters. Doubtless, they are sometimes sorely tried. I have known headmasters whom I would willingly have sent to the death of a thousand cuts, administrative or financial. And, of course, they have a duty to ensure that public money is properly spent. But some of the stories I hear from some of my colleagues in maintained schools would make the angels weep—if angels have any interest in educational freedom.

I do not want to seem to condemn all educational administrators for the shortcomings of some of them; and I salute with gratitude the many among them who are liberal-minded, energetic, and idealistic. But we are concerned here with educational freedom; and it must be recorded that many administrators do not approach their schools and their teachers from this point of view at all. The free life of their schools is not their aim. And until it is, for all schools at all levels, they are, in my submission, coming at their job from the wrong end.

They are, indeed, the servants of their committees, and those committees are not always either wise or well-informed. I have, earlier, referred to this element in the present educational situation, and I will not labour it. Only, I would appeal to all men and women who have the interests of children at heart to make time, in their own busy lives, for service to education in this way, so that, above all, party-political considerations may not determine questions which affect the lives and happiness of millions of children every day.

Now, in conclusion, I must try to make clear one point which may seem to be at variance with what I have said so far. Teachers in this country are not servants of the State. They are appointed, paid, and if need arise, dismissed by a local education authority. Consequently, in spite of the growing habit of appointing a teacher to the service of an authority, instead of to a school, with the possibility of 'posting' to some uncongenial job, and in spite of the vagaries of some of the authorities, we do not suffer from regimentation from the centre. The disillusioned sometimes wish that we did; for they would feel safer if they were under control more distant than that which comes from the office in the Town Hall. But at least we do not provide material for any such boast as that of the Minister of Public Instruction who could tell a visitor which page of which text-book all the children in the State schools were studying at ten o'clock on a Tuesday morning. That is not the English way. Rather we find ourselves in a partnership, empirically working itself out, not laid down on any abstract *a priori* principles, a partnership in which everybody concerned with education is daily engaged, whether he be parent, teacher, administrator, governor, civil servant or—most important of all—child. If we plead for freedom, if we cry, in despair, in anger, or in defiance 'Set the teacher free' it is only because we desire that freedom as a means to a further end—'Set the children free'. For they are the end of all our labours.

5

The International Aspect of Education

SIR JOHN MAUD

THE world is shrinking, we are often told. And so it is. With each improvement in the means of movement and communication we find ourselves living at closer quarters. But as *the* world becomes smaller, *my* world becomes bigger. Fifty years ago it was common enough to find, say, a Lancashireman who had never been to London. His world was the village or town where he lived and the country within some fifty miles of it. Living and moving in that world of a few thousand souls, it was not difficult for him to be, and feel himself to be, of some significance. For his son, living and moving in a world limited to-day neither by the Channel nor by the Atlantic, it is not difficult to feel a thing of no significance whatever.

That the world has become, and is becoming, larger for each of the 2,000 million people who inhabit it, and that in consequence each one of them is under a stronger temptation to feel dwarfed, without individual significance or power of personal action—'a stranger and afraid, in a world I never made'—this is a fact of far greater moment to the educator than the complementary fact that the world is getting smaller.

How can we learn to be, and feel ourselves to be, persons, and persons of unique significance, in a world of 2,000 million persons? How can we arm our children against the danger of feeling ciphers as they become aware of the hugeness of the world, and of the probability that it will be half as huge again in 25 years' time? First, surely, by contriving that in the earlier stages of growing up they find themselves members of reasonably small communities—that, besides their own homes, they have schools and clubs and colleges of such a size and character that the children have some chance of learning the elements of the art of living, and letting live, as persons among other persons.

The second requirement is that this artificial community, the school, should be closely linked with its natural counterpart, the family—that teachers and parents should be in conscious and continuous alliance.

It follows, as a third requirement, that when we decide that some public authority must become responsible for organizing schools (or the schools we need will not be organized at all), it should be an authority responsible to the local people rather than to some geographically more extensive community.

Now in Great Britian—indeed, in the English-speaking world—a strong tradition has been established that a *local* authority should be responsible for ensuring that parents, whatever their income, can discharge their responsibility for the education of their children. So in England and Wales to-day we have 146 local education authorities, the county and the county borough councils who are charged with the duty of securing the provision of education suitable to the 'age, ability and aptitude' of all the children of their respective areas whose parents do not choose to educate them suitably in some other way.

But in Britain, as in any other nation State, the several parts of the country differ more or less notably one from another, not only in spirit but in economic strength. And, apart from such differences, none of them is likely to contain within its own borders the teaching and other professional resources which its children need if they are all to receive the education appropriate to each. Further, the wider community of the nation is interested in the education of all the children in the land. On its own behalf as a nation, and on behalf of each individual child, it is entitled to insist that certain standards shall be reached by all the smaller communities responsible for educating their local children.

In Britain, therefore, we have willed that local authorities should have primary, but not sole, responsibility for education.

And we have willed the means, as well as the end, in the form of an ingenious administrative system which has evolved over the last hundred years.

The citizens of, say, Merthyr Tydfil are primarily responsible for education in Merthyr Tydfil. But their fellow citizens in the richer parts of England and Wales help them substantially to pay for it—70 per cent. of their approved expenditure on education is paid back to them by the Ministry of Education out of general taxation collected over the whole country. We pay local rates as neighbours to the local children, and we pay national taxes as neighbours to the children of England and Wales.

On the same principle, the Ministry of Education neither appoints nor dismisses the teachers: that is left to the local authority. But there are national standards of qualification and a national pension scheme for all teachers, whatever school or local authority they serve.

The Ministry builds no school or college; but it sets a minimum standard in the building regulations. It prescribes no text-book or syllabus or teaching method; but through His Majesty's Inspectors and through the various publications of the Ministry the experience of the best schools, teachers, and authorities is made generally available and the laggards are goaded or cajoled.

At the best (and nowadays most of the time) there is a working partnership between those who represent the local and those who represent the national community—as there should also be between teachers and those who 'minister' to teachers, as part of the local or of the central administration. But at the worst there are sanctions whereby the Minister can direct, by word or by deed (that is, by withholding grant), a local authority which fails in his opinion to carry out the national policy for education.

Local authorities, with chief but not sole responsibility, and a Ministry of Education, able to help, especially with money, and in the last resort to compel: these are the twin means whereby in England and Wales we seek the end of assuring for our children, whether they live in rich or poor parts of the country, the kind of education which will enable each one of them to reach the height of his personal stature.

We cannot here consider how well or ill this system works, nor how it has come to be established. But its existence implies three convictions. Firstly, we want a community much smaller, and therefore more intimate, than the nation to be immediately responsible for the public service of educating our children. Secondly, as a national community we want to supplement, financially and professionally, the best educational effort that the local community can make. And thirdly, we believe that we have discovered administrative techniques for attempting to satisfy both these wishes simultaneously.

In the United States only the first of these three convictions has hitherto found expression in the public system of education. The Federal Government is unable to supplement financially the educational efforts of the States, for the Congress has so far declined to legislate on any such lines as those proposed by the President in the Federal Aid Bill which has been under discussion in recent years. One consequence of this difference between the two countries is that huge disparities in educational opportunity still exist between one part of the United States and another, such as cannot be paralleled in Great Britain. One reason for the difference is the inability of the citizens of the United States, with their heterogeneous multitude of cultural traditions, to reach a sufficient measure of agreement on the proper place of religion in a public system of education.

But difficult though it may be, in a country with the size and history of the United States, to extend the bounds of the educational community as far as the national frontier, that frontier must itself be transcended if the citizens living within it are to be fully educated.

The world is divided geographically into nation States, as Britain is divided into counties and cities; but in comparison with what the inhabitants of most counties and cities of Britain feel about each other, in no nation can the citizens be said to have either the will to help and be helped by other nationals in matters of education, or the administrative means to give effect to any such will if it existed.

And yet it is ludicrous to suppose that any one nation, rich or poor, developed or under-developed, is capable in isolation from other nations, of discharging its educational duty towards its own nationals. No Englishman can become an adequate teacher of a modern language—or perhaps of modern history either—without some first-hand acquaintance with the continent of Europe. Much the same can be said of the French. So neither English nor French children can be properly educated unless personal contact is made, at the best, between themselves and the other country or at least between their teachers and the other country. And nowadays, because of currency and other limitations on free movement across frontiers, this happens only when both the people themselves and their respective Governments take the necessary steps.

And of course it is not only the formal education of children that calls for some crossing of the frontier. At the university level there is still more obvious need for this—indeed, for the re-creation, in modern terms, of such conditions as were characteristic of medieval Europe and enabled the wandering scholar to pass naturally from the universities of one country to those of another and thereafter to obtain, if he were good enough, the right to teach in any of them. But apart altogether from scholastic education and the advancement of learning, are creative artists likely to come to the height of their genius as painters, sculptors, writers, or musicians if their life, and especially their early life, has to be spent exclusively in their own country and if other artists come seldom from abroad as strangers in their midst? It seems hardly less unlikely that ordinary men and women will well discharge their democratic responsibilities as citizens if they remain ignorant of all facts, other than those observable within the frontier of their own nation, which are to-day relevant to the world problems (for they are world problems, insoluble by nations in isolation) of food, raw materials, employment, and security.

It is perhaps less easy for us in Britain to appreciate that this is true of ourselves than to recognize its application to the people of the United States or of the U.S.S.R. We need no great imagination to realize the importance, to the rest of the world, either of the picture of world events outside Russia presented to the citizens of the U.S.S.R. by the Russian authorities through every medium of education, or of the 'adult education' movement of the last ten years in the United States —a movement which has already made Lend-Lease and Marshall Aid politically possible in a country thousands of miles from Europe which thirty years ago was unready to join the League of Nations.

On the other hand, a nation's need of economic, as distinct from professional, help from beyond its frontier, for educational as for other purposes, is more easily recognized by its own nationals than by those of the richer nations from whom the help might come. Thus, the economic help from outside Nigeria which the Nigerians need at the present stage in their educational development is perhaps more obvious to them than to the British taxpayer. And the same is true of the great majority of that two-thirds of the world's population that must to-day be described as illiterate. 'How can the vicious circle be broken without help from the more highly developed countries?' these Africans and Indians and Indonesians and Burmese may well ask. 'Until we can afford to train thousands of teachers and pay them a livelihood when trained, we shall remain illiterate and incapable of improving our agriculture or developing the other potential resources of our under-developed countries. But so long as our countries remain under-developed, we cannot afford education.'

Nevertheless, for a variety of reasons one nation often feels a strong interest in another nation's education. One reason is fear. The victorious allies have a strong interest in German and Japanese education. Again, for fear of communism some of those allies are deeply interested in the education of others; and those others, for fear of capitalism, are not uninterested in education beyond their own national boundaries. Hunger is a more positive interest than fear; and since the war desire for groundnuts (to take one example) has powerfully re-inforced our other motives for investing British taxpayers' capital in African education.

Sometimes in alliance with these self-interested motives of fear and hunger (and sometimes not), man's conscience also drives him on occasion beyond the national frontier to be his brother's educator. The Christian and the communist missionary are equally good examples. Whatever the mixture of motives may be, great efforts are nowadays deliberately made to educate our neighbours abroad. The 'Voice of America' is one example; Russian and British broadcasts are others in the same medium. Far more potent probably, though less deliberate, is the influence of American and other films. And many of the activities of the British Council come under the same category.

Thus nations not only feel a need that other nations should help them, both professionally and by economic means, to discharge their educational duties to their own nationals: nations also feel anxious, for various reasons, to participate in one another's educational work. As in Great Britain first but not sole responsibility for education rests with the local authority, so it would seem that in the modern world as a whole first but not sole responsibility rests with the nation. But in so far as nations wish their national deficiencies in education to be made up by foreign aid, and are prepared to help to make up the deficiencies of other nations, how can such wishes be met in practice?

The methods used by the Allies in Germany are of course exceptional. From the outset Allied policy assumed that as soon as possible education of Germans must again become a responsibility of Germans, and chiefly of Germans organized in *local* communities. And as early as 1948 education passed from the Control Commission into the hands of the German provincial and county authorities, with allied education officers acting only as advisers. But so long as ultimate political sovereignty rests with the Allies, the mutual relationship of

Germans and foreigners remains inevitably abnormal, even in respect of education.

Between us in Britain and our 65 million fellow citizens in the Colonial Empire another 'abnormal' relationship exists, in education as in other respects. Here again our policy is based on the principle of local responsibility: the Uganda Government, for example, is primarily responsible for education in Uganda. But until that Government becomes solely responsible to the people of Uganda, there is a constitutional link, through the Secretary of State for the Colonies, between the Uganda Government and the British Parliament and people— exemplified, under one aspect, in the financial contribution of British taxpayers to the Colonial Development and Welfare Fund, and under another aspect in the British members of the Uganda Education Service who are still recruited through the Colonial Office.

But in the mutual relationship which has recently developed in education between, say, Britain and France, there is much evidence of what two nations can do to help each other without infringing the national sovereignty of either State or, in Britain, the limited sovereignty of teachers and local education authorities respectively. Nowadays every year five or six hundred secondary schools in Britain have on their staffs an *assistant* from France, and there are nearly half as many French schools with British *assistants*. Every year a very large number of British and French school-children come into personal contact, through visits to each other's countries or through correspondence. Each year since 1946 British teachers of French have spent some time in Paris on 'refresher' courses and there is a scheme under which some of them can supplement their two-year training in British colleges by a special one-year course at the Sorbonne. British Science teachers had courses in France in 1948 and Norway in 1949. There are similar examples of recent collaboration between Britain and Norway, Denmark, Holland, Italy, Germany, and Austria—a course for British teachers in Rome; another in Germany with German teachers; a visit to Britain of School Inspectors from the other four countries who signed the Brussels Treaty (to be repeated subsequently in the other countries). And meanwhile larger numbers of children are learning a second modern language in British schools than at any previous time in our history. Indeed, under the Education Act of 1944 Britain is now for the first time committed to the principle that every child should have the opportunity to learn a second language, as part of the new concept of 'secondary education for all'.

But since 1945 Britain has been committed to another new principle: that in addition to arrangements made directly between the schools and teachers and education authorities of two or more countries, a single inter-governmental organization is needed for educational, scientific, and cultural collaboration between all the nations of the world whose Governments are prepared to accept certain defined conditions of membership. On this principle Britain, and some fifty other countries, are now members of a specialized agency of the United Nations, known by the initials U.N.E.S.C.O.—the United Nations Educational, Scientific and Cultural Organization.

(These fifty member States include Czechoslovakia, Poland, and Hungary, but Russia and the other countries of eastern Europe have never joined.)

It is only through its government that a nation may seek membership of Unesco; it is the government of each nation that appoints the representatives who meet in General Conference each year (at the headquarters in Paris, or elsewhere, say in Mexico City, Beirut or Florence) to decide how much money Unesco shall spend and on what activities; each nation's contribution to the annual budget is collected by its government by taxation and then handed over for Unesco to spend. Thus our membership of Unesco implies no formal abrogation of national sovereignty: it is first through their government that the specialists (the educators, scientists, writers, artists, film-producers, broadcasters, newspapermen) and the non-specialists (children, adults, taxpayers, members of Churches,

Trade Unions and all other such organizations) are represented in this new international institution.

But those original government-appointed representatives who drafted the constitution believed that some other means, to supplement representation through national governments, should be devised in each State member of Unesco, whereby the *people* of each nation (and in particular those with a special interest in education, science, and culture) might be associated with their government in the work of the organization. Accordingly, in the United States a National Commission of a hundred members (of whom 90 would be appointed by the Educational, Scientific, and Cultural institutions of the country) was established by the Congress; and its influence on the Federal Government quickly, and increasingly, proved formidable in shaping United States participation in Unesco's work. In Britain a National Commission has evolved, with similar purpose but on different lines, which now consists of some 250 members (all private citizens, with two or three exceptions) organized in a series of specialist 'Co-operating Bodies' for education, the natural and social sciences, museums, libraries, the arts, the means of mass communication and other subjects.

The fact remains, however, that Unesco is a society of sovereign states, formed for certain wide but limited purposes. Historically, the first of such creations was the International Labour Organization, established after the First World War, for a different purpose but in much the same way as was Unesco after the second. The Food and Agriculture Organization (F.A.O.) was the first specialized agency of the United Nations to be established, shortly before Unesco; and now there are several others—the World Health Organization (W.H.O.) for example. All are loosely linked with each other and with the United Nations Organization itself, by various means and in particular through U.N.O.'s Economic and Social Council. But each has its own constitution, its own membership of States, its own budget and secretariat. It is therefore as if the counties and county boroughs of Great Britain were sovereign authorities, with absolute financial autonomy and no Parliament or Departments of State to exercise authority on the nation's behalf; and as if some, but not all, of them had established Ministries of Labour, of Food and Agriculture, of Health, of Education, Science, and Culture, without being prepared to abandon their local sovereignty or establish any single authority, federal or unitary, for the whole of Great Britain. That is the kind of institution which fifty nations have created by their decision to belong to Unesco.

What Unesco can hope to do, then, in the present state of world opinion and international organization is fundamentally different from what would be possible if nations were related one to another as local education authorities are actually related in Britain to-day. In no country can Unesco do anything to which the national government objects.

There are no 'sanctions' for Unesco to apply against a nation, however far it may seem to fall below the standards which its government has agreed to set itself in accepting the constitution of Unesco. That constitution, for example, clearly implies that educational opportunity should be available equally to both sexes and without discrimination against anyone on grounds of race or creed. But if anyone wished to raise the question whether communists and non-communists enjoyed equal opportunities for education in Czechoslovakia, Poland, and Hungary, or Jews in the Arab States, or women in Egypt, or native Africans in the Union of South Africa, or negroes in parts of the United States, there would be difficulty in even discussing the question at a Unesco Conference, and if it were discussed, no effective action could follow without the consent of the responsible national government. Indeed, the constitution specifically excludes action on any matter that falls within the domestic jurisdiction of any member State. Nevertheless, despite this limitation, the very existence of Unesco offers the governments and peoples of fifty nations an opportunity to behave as members of a wider society than the nation and to take common action in educational, scientific, and cultural affairs.

The procedure of this wider society is based on well-established democratic principles. Decisions about the size of the annual budget and how it shall be spent can be taken by a simple majority of the States represented at a general conference; each national delegation has one vote, and none has a veto. The organization has agreed that each member State shall contribute a percentage of the annual budget of Unesco which is calculated on a scale agreed by the United Nations Organization itself and designed on the principle of contribution according to ability to pay. Thus the United States at present contribute 38·93 per cent. of the year's budget, the United Kingdom 13·83 per cent., France 7·29 per cent., and Haiti 0·05 per cent.

Amendments of the Constitution and decisions to recommend formal Conventions for governmental ratification cannot be made by simple majority vote. And of course there is a procedure whereby a member State may resign from the Organization (just as Russia resigned from the World Health Organization). But broadly speaking the general conference can decide to raise and spend money on any action of an educational, scientific, or cultural kind which seems good to a majority of the delegations.

On such decisions there are in practice limitations of two main kinds: first, the readiness of public opinion to give and to receive assistance across national frontiers; and secondly the adequacy of administrative means to enable such assistance to be given and received. The combined effect of these limitations is perhaps most simply shown by the size of the annual budget, which for the year 1950 amounts to $8 million (equivalent to £2·9 million at the current exchange rate) and may be compared with $7·8 million, $7·7 million, and $6·0 million for the years 1949, 1948, and 1947 respectively.

During these early years in the life of Unesco, however ready public opinion in the main contributing countries might have been to support a larger budget, it is extremely unlikely that people of high enough administrative and technical quality could have been found in sufficient numbers to staff the Secretariat, both at the headquarters of Unesco and in the member States, which would have been needed if a budget substantially larger than that actually voted was to be well spent. Past experience strongly suggests that the pace of future progress will depend on the interaction of these two developments: the increase of men's desire to treat each other as neighbours across their national boundaries, and the growth of administrative ability to enable that desire to be expressed in action.

Meanwhile it would be quite unrealistic to suppose that in the next few years Unesco will have much more money to spend than it has at present. What conclusions follow from this assumption? Here British educational experience of the last hundred years is perhaps relevant—and encouraging.

In 1833 the national Government first voted money for education—a tiny sum, to be spent by voluntary religious organizations on their local schools, but it was the thin end of an enormous wedge. The tradition of using public funds to help 'private' educational enterprise became established and was easily extended to cover 'public' enterprise when locally elected education authorities came later into existence to fill the gaps left by the voluntary organizations. And with this tradition there naturally grew the complementary one, that central government should concern itself with the education provided by local authorities, whether private or public, who received public money. Thus national standards were gradually established. His Majesty's Inspectors of Schools came gradually to be recognized as a source of professional help to the teachers (in the schools themselves, at refresher courses, and through publications), alongside the financial help provided with slowly increasing generosity by central government to supplement the economic resources of the local authorities. Thus a national system of education slowly came into existence, in response to the twin development of a national desire that all children should have educational opportunities however poor their parents or the local community where they lived, and of administrative methods whereby the rights of the local authority could be respected and its deficiencies at the same time made good from national resources.

In some such way Unesco is becoming an international system whereby the State members may supplement their educational, scientific, and cultural efforts and make good some of their individual deficiencies.

The method of the financial grant-in-aid has been used by Unesco from the outset with excellent results. Associations of natural scientists of various kinds have been helped in this way to renew their activities after the interruptions of the war; international scientific conferences have been held which would not have been held without Unesco's intervention, and scientists have been enabled to attend them who could not otherwise have afforded their fare. In other fields of learning new international associations have been formed with the necessary funds and secretarial assistance supplied by Unesco in the early stages (the International Council of Philosophy and Humanistic Studies is an example). And in the field of the arts, the International Theatre Institute and the International Council of Music have been established by pioneers in several countries with the stimulus and support of grants and personal assistance from Unesco.

But besides encouraging voluntary international effort in these ways, as the national Government has encouraged voluntary effort within Great Britain for the last hundred years, Unesco has also learnt to employ internationally the techniques of the educational mission, the refresher course, and publications. Nothing comparable to His Majesty's Inspectorate has been created; but on the invitation of the Governments of Afghanistan, the Philippines, and Siam, Unesco has obtained the services of educational experts from various countries and sent them, at Unesco's expense, as educational missions to advise those governments. Again, it has organized international seminars (at Sèvres, Ashridge, Elsinore, Rio, in Mysore and at McGill) where experts in some particular educational field have come together from many countries and worked as a group for several weeks, exchanging experience and advancing their subject (the training of teachers, for example, or rural adult education). Again, through a publication such as *Study Abroad* Unesco has made generally available for the first time information about the thousands of opportunities for graduate or post-graduate work offered by educational institutions throughout the world to suitable men and women of other nations.

These are some of the ways by which Unesco has already achieved results and helped the fruitful movement of people, ideas, and materials about the world. It has proved that, internationally as well as nationally, bureaucrats can minister effectively to some of the needs of teachers, scientists, and even artists, and that such collaboration is specially needed in a world cabined and confined within currency and customs barriers. It has proved that even in the present state of world opinion an inter-governmental organization is needed and can succeed—at least in enabling nations to make good some of their *professional* deficiencies in education: those that correspond to the needs of teachers and local authorities in Britain which a national Ministry of Education can help to meet, through an advisory service and by other means, at relatively modest expense.

But Unesco has also found itself committed to the more ambitious task of seeking to modify the appalling disparities of educational opportunity at present open to people of different nations. And here too it has had some measure of success. From the first it has set as one of its chief objectives the educational reconstruction of areas that suffered most from the war. It has accepted as inevitable that its own direct relief work could do no more than supplement, on a small scale, the reconstruction work of other agencies. Its chief purpose has therefore been to assess the needs, bring them to the notice of those who might find supplies to meet them, and ease the process of matching demand with supply.

It is a fact (however much or little credit may be due to Unesco) that since Unesco set its hand to this work goods and services worth several times the whole Unesco budget, have been contributed by voluntary subscribers (mainly in the United States, but also in Australia, New Zealand, Canada, Norway, and Britain) to educational reconstruction in eastern and western

Europe, in the Near East (especially for Arab refugee children), and in Asia. Such relief work will always be needed, in consequence, if not of war, of such catastrophes of nature as earthquakes in Ecuador. And each time the need is met it will be because men are capable of recognizing one another across the world as neighbours and coming to one another's help.

But can this happen except under the stimulus of dramatic and exceptional necessity? Will men in more developed countries give time and money to the 'fundamental education' of the illiterate two-thirds of mankind? A fraction of Unesco's budget is in fact spent on precisely this kind of international neighbourliness: on a 'pilot project', for example, in Haiti where Unesco and several other specialized agencies of the United Nations have proved that they can work together to raise standards in an under-developed area. But the amount of money at present available to Unesco is totally inadequate for more than exploratory work. In contrast to the present position inside Britain, where the financial resources of all local education authorities are supplemented from national taxation to the extent of some two-thirds of their expenditure (the proportion varying widely according to the economic strength of the area), the position in the society of nations constituting Unesco is that each nation is still almost completely dependent on its local resources for educational development.

Following the proposal made in 1949 by President Truman in the 'Fourth Point' of his address to the Congress, all the United Nations agencies have been elaborating co-ordinated plans for bringing 'technical assistance' to under-developed countries that ask for it. Under this plan Unesco will find considerably greater opportunity for its work in fundamental education: it will have a supplementary budget to finance new schemes, say for the training of teachers, administrators, and other nationals of the under-developed countries, both by bringing them to be trained in Great Britain, the United States, and other countries and by sending out nationals of these latter countries to help in their training on the spot.

This technical assistance plan may prove to be more valuable than any other work so far undertaken by the United Nations: Unesco has rightly devoted much of the energies of its best men to participation in the plan ever since the first proposals were made. But education is desperately expensive, and there is no short cut to its development anywhere. The illiterate regions of the world cannot be properly educated unless they become more wealthy, and that most of them cannot become unless they are enabled by the wealthier nations to develop their agriculture, industry, and trade. Unesco can hope only to help in relatively minor ways towards this end: the achievement of its educational purpose depends largely on the growth of economic and political common sense throughout the world and on the success of the other United Nations agencies.

Sir Kenneth Clark in *Landscape into Art* has drawn attention to the new worlds of time and space revealed by the microscope and the telescope. 'The snug and sensible nature' he writes, 'which we can see with our own eyes has ceased to satisfy our imaginations.' 'What should we do, then?' he asks, and continues: 'We can contrive to *forget* these fantastic, incredible facts in front of a fine prospect, just as we can forget the starvation in the world in front of a good dinner. But the creation of great works of art must rest on something more than this salutary animal accommodation to the responses of the moment.'

We can forget the millions of African and Asiatic illiterates, in front of our own black-listed schools or the prospect of a million more children to educate in British schools in 1953 than were there to educate in 1947—or, for that matter, in face of the claims and satisfaction of a life of learning, in an ancient university. But education must rest on something sounder than make-believe. And if we face the facts of 1950, there are only two broad alternatives before us.

The first is the eventual destruction of the human spirit by creeping uniformity—by progressive obliteration of the differences between nation and nation, between East and West, between cultures, tastes, and individuals. We need not speculate on the stages whereby this might happen. One of the early symptoms would be the flooding of those parts of the world which were not yet able to produce their own films or broadcasts or to employ their own news agencies by films, broadcasts, and news produced elsewhere: to some extent this has begun already, in parts of Europe, and there will continue to be danger of its happening on a much larger scale so long as the power to use the new means of mass communication is so unequally distributed among the various nations.

This is the alternative towards which any totalitarian régime leads those subjected to it—and in the modern world there is no territorial limit beyond which a totalitarian régime will not, sooner or later, wish to extend its influence, whether for reasons of positive missionary zeal or simply from fear. But the danger is not only from the conscientious totalitarian. Western industrialism is quite capable of producing similar results, without any deliberate wish to do so. And so long as world peace continues to depend on the possession of preponderant power by those who want peace, it will be a precarious peace, and the world will continue to be in mortal danger of forcible reduction to uniformity—if not to ashes.

But we must believe that there is a second alternative: a world in which national and cultural loyalties are found to be as compatible with membership of a world society as is family loyalty with membership of a local or national society. Such a world is at present almost infinitely remote. We have only to note the weakness of our present sense of membership even of a western European Society—let alone the remoteness of any society embracing eastern and western Europe. But there is encouragement in the relationship of new and old Dominions, Asiatic and Anglo-Saxon, within the British Commonwealth to-day, when we consider how fanciful the very idea seemed ten years ago, and in the new readiness of the United States to involve itself in Europe and the world.

And whatever the prospect of success or failure, there is no escape now from the effort to make real this idea of a world society—either for the Christian or the democrat, or indeed for anyone who declines either to pretend that his world is limited by the national frontier or to lose himself in the inhumanity of innumerable masses.

Education (in the sense of what happens to people in schools and colleges and in their contact with books, newspapers, films, broadcasts, and the rest) has only an indirect and eventual influence on the movement of the world in one or other of these directions. The precariousness of the peace and the danger of war depend, in the short run, on economic and political decisions, and these in turn depend rather on *past* 'education' than on anything which educators can do now. But clearly the long-term prospects of making real the idea of a world society depend more on education than on anything else. The world, therefore, has a strong interest in education: that is to say, if we think of ourselves and succeeding generations as people who inhabit or will inhabit one physical world, and who desire neither uniformity nor chaos, we have much to hope or fear from what happens to education.

And what from this point of view we have reason to hope from education is precisely what we also have reason to hope from it if we consider the individual interest of our own children and other persons young and old. Children need, first and foremost, education in their own homes, where each is most likely to be recognized as unique but where each has also rights and obligations within the family. But even the largest family is too small, and even the happiest family inadequate, for the purpose of a complete education. So the larger, deliberately contrived community of the school is needed, where the child can continue to be treated as unique (in ability and aptitude, as well as age) but where he can learn that uniqueness is compatible with membership of a group larger and more heterogeneous than the family. And the local community of neighbouring families offers the best means of providing such schools where without communal provision they would not be provided. But the local education authority by its very nature is subject to certain limitations; it is too small and too poor to carry the whole responsibility. And so the national community is needed, not to

G

replace but to respect and supplement the local authority and the local schools and colleges.

But what is true of the local community is true also of the national. The national frontiers are in some respects too wide for educational purposes, and therefore the local area needs to be used; but they are in other respects too narrow, and therefore the national communities must help each other to make good their own professional and economic deficiencies.

Thus, thinking only of the individual's educational need, we find ourselves requiring a pattern of educational provision which includes the family, the school, the local and national authorities —and something more. And this is the educational pattern which seems also most likely to foster the growth of a world society.

The extension of the sense of neighbourliness beyond the frontier means two things. First, increased readiness, on the part of nations and specialists of each nation, to help and be helped by one another—in other words a more imaginative awareness of common interest. And secondly, increased respect for the right and duty of national groups to be different and distinctive, and a corresponding increase in tolerance.

If education is regarded primarily as a means of leading other men to do what I want (for example, to produce groundnuts for the use of British housewives) or of preventing them from doing what I fear (for example, starting another war in Europe, or joining the communist party), then it is idle to pretend that educational development can be expected to extend the sense of neighbourliness as described above.

But if such ends as those are what we intend to achieve by education, we should beware of results that belie our expectation. However clearly men may envisage the types they want produced by education, they had better be prepared for disappointment.

You may seek to justify the country's educational expenditure by reference to the country's need to export more goods; but do not be surprised if some poets and artists whose contribution to the export drive must be neglected emerge from the schools. You may believe with passion that education is needed to save people from becoming communists, or racialists; but you must be prepared for precisely opposite results. Indeed, it is even rash to assume that as people of different countries learn more about each other, they will necessarily like each other more. (Ask any infantryman of the first world war who fought in the trenches and sampled the varied sanitary arrangements there what he thinks of the allies and enemies who were respectively responsible.)

The only motive for promoting education which has any reasonable chance of success is the motive which impels us to educate our own children—the desire that by education the child or adult will learn to make up his mind for himself and so become a man of significance, able to hold his own against the worst that modern or future batteries of mass suggestion and propaganda can do to subdue his individual judgement, neither a stranger in the world nor afraid of it, but aware of his power, however limited, to co-operate in the fashioning and re-fashioning of it.

And if we desire this for our own children, can we reasonably either decline to desire it for our neighbours' children or maintain that our neighbours live only this side of the national frontier? 'No man is an island entire of itself. . . . Any man's death diminishes me, for I am involved in mankind. And therefore never send to know for whom the bell tolls: it tolls for thee.' If we believe John Donne was right in that confession, we must believe also that any man's *ignorance* diminishes me and that we are responsible for every man's enlightenment.

But whether we are persuaded of that or unpersuaded, our own children cannot be fully educated unless men of other nations are so persuaded and help us to educate them.

At present it cannot be expected that more than a small minority in any nation will be prepared to act on this belief—a minority of the citizens, of course, but a minority also of the teachers, artists, scientists, and men of learning. On these minorities, within each nation and within each international community of educational, scientific, and cultural specialists, depend the prospects both of education and of a world society worthy of the name.

6

The Scientific Background to Educational Change

REX KNIGHT

In a single lecture it would clearly be impossible to survey the *whole* scientific background of *all* educational change. I propose, therefore, to limit my treatment of the subject in two directions. First, I shall refer only to educational changes that have occurred since 1893, the year when James Sully founded the British Association for Child Study, which marked the beginning of modern educational research in Great Britain. Secondly, in describing the scientific background of these changes, I shall refer only to the contributions of psychology, which is the science principally concerned and the only one with which I am qualified to deal.

Many important educational changes have had no scientific background. Unlike most developments in medicine, they have not resulted from the practical application of facts and principles revealed by research. Some have been due to changes in our circumstances, or our ruling political, social, and educational ideals; others have reflected the views, not necessarily scientific, of forceful Advisory Committees and individuals.

One such change has been the repeated raising of the school-leaving age, which in England was 11 in 1893, 12 in 1899, 14 in 1902, and 15 in 1947. None of these extensions of the compulsory school age was the result of investigations into the effects of different periods of schooling on different groups of children. They all took place simply because a large number of people, and a majority of members of Parliament, thought that every child should stay longer at school. No doubt most of those who proposed or supported each extension believed that it would be of benefit, and what they believed may have well been true; but they formed their belief, and based their action, on evidence that was not scientific.

A second change that has had no scientific background is the great increase in the number of entries and passes in the School Certificate and Higher Certificate Examinations. In 1938 77,010 candidates sat the School Certificate Examination, and 58,848 were successful; in 1947 the corresponding figures were 107,356 and 80,672. There was an even greater rise in the figures for the Higher Certificate Examinations. In 1938 13,202 candidates were presented, and 9,514 passed; in 1947 the corresponding figures were 26,322 and 18,701, which means that the sixth forms in the grammar schools throughout England had doubled in numbers during the previous decade. This remarkable change cannot be said to have been due to the activities of psychologists or other scientists, though it undoubtedly confirms the views of psychologists like Burt who long ago produced evidence to show that many children who had sufficient intelligence to pass these examinations left school before they could sit them.

A third development that has not emerged from scientific research is the striking change in the content of secondary education. This process has sometimes been described as one in which the old 'unitary' curriculum, which was supposed to provide a general education, has disintegrated into a chaotic collection of subjects; and certainly the number of subjects taught in secondary schools has greatly increased during the past fifty years. The most conspicuous of the new courses are those that constitute technical education; but, despite the assurance of the Spens and Norwood Committees that the traditional distinction in value between 'liberal' and 'technical' education is unsound, it is clear that the 'parity of esteem' now claimed for technical subjects is not held to be justified primarily by their educational value. The *Spens Report* thought it well to remind us that in France during the Second Empire 'it was urged that the country required more industrialists and engineers, who might be prepared by a scientific course, and fewer journalists and lawyers produced by a training that was mainly literary'.

Similarly, the *White Paper on Educational Reconstruction* urged that England now 'cannot afford to rest content with a system under which the technical education of its potential skilled workers, industrial leaders, or commercial executives is left so largely to the initiative of the young employees themselves'. Clearly, in such arguments as these, the extension of technical education is being proposed, not on educational grounds, but for the sake of national efficiency and prosperity.

Accompanying the inclusion of technical courses and other new subjects in the curriculum, there has been a striking change in the subjects chosen by candidates for the Higher Certificate Examination. We have seen that the number of entries for this examination almost exactly doubled between 1938 and 1947. But this twofold increase in the total number of candidates was not reflected in the number of those who entered for Latin or Greek or ancient history (indeed, the number of entries for Greek fell from 881 to 741); and it was barely reflected in the number who took English or history. In mathematics, on the other hand, the entries increased from 5,500 to 12,800, in physics from 4,000 to 10,500, in chemistry from 3,900 to 9,800, in botany from 757 to 2,123, and there were similar increases in biology, zoology, and economics. Here again, what has happened must be ascribed, not to psychological or other research, but to changes in our national condition and outlook, and to the changed ambitions of children and parents, who have naturally been affected by the growing power and prestige of the sciences and the better prospects of employment in some branch of technology.

A fourth educational change that owes nothing to science has been the establishment of the three types of secondary school; the grammar school, the technical school, and the modern school. The only connexion between psychologists and this innovation is that they have vigorously attacked the ground on which it was recommended by the Norwood Committee. Thus they have pointed out that there is no evidence for the suggestion that a definite stage of growth begins at about the age of eleven, or for the crucial statement that the three types of school correspond to three distinct types of mind, clearly discernible among children of eleven. The *Norwood Report* defines the three types of mind in these terms; the grammar-school type 'is interested in learning for its own sake; it can take in an argument or a piece of connected reasoning; it is interested in causes, in the relatedness of related things, in a coherent body of knowledge; it is willing to suspend judgment and to be detached in attitude'; the technical-school type is one 'whose interests and abilities lie markedly in the field of applied science or applied art; he often has an uncanny insight into the intricacies of mechanism, whereas the subtleties of language instruction are too delicate for him'; and the modern-school type is one 'who deals more easily with concrete things than with ideas; who often fails to relate his knowledge or skill to other branches of activity; who, because he is interested only in the moment, may be incapable of a long series of connected steps'.

Burt and Schonell are only two of the psychologists who have exposed the fallacies underlying this strange excursion into typology. Schonell refers to it as 'perhaps the most outstanding example' of the fact that in British education 'too often and too strongly does mere opinion hold the field instead of information gathered from observation and experiment'. Undoubtedly, the Norwood Committee made a gross error in suggesting that boys who are 'interested in the relatedness of related things' are unsuited to applied science, and that boys who possess 'an uncanny insight into the intricacies of mechanism' are floored by French. Evidently unaware of the many researches that show that human intellectual abilities are positively correlated, the Norwood Committee blithely overlooked the fact that the individual who is above average in one respect is on that account more likely, not less likely, to be above average in other respects. It also seems to have supposed that the interests of children of eleven are assessable and fixed, and either that special aptitudes and interests always go together, or that a definition is not impaired if it treats independent variables as though they were concomitant. Six years ago, Burt, having set out the evidence that conflicts with the 'mere opinion' of the

Norwood Committee, concluded: 'Any scheme of organization which proposes to classify children at the age of eleven or twelve according to qualitative mental types rather than to general intelligence, is in conflict with the known facts of psychology.' Nothing has happened in the last six years to modify this conclusion. Alexander to be sure, has firmly told us that 'whatever disagreement there may be on the validity and reliability with which children can be allocated at 11+, it must be recognized that it is an immediate administrative necessity that the task should be undertaken; the essential need, therefore, is to make available at once the most effective practical procedure in the fulfilment of that task'. But it is difficult to see how even 'administrative necessity' can lead us to discern the indiscernible, and to find three types of mind that do not exist.

There are other educational changes which have had a scientific background but have not been primarily due to psychology. One example is the great improvement in the design of school buildings and equipment during the past fifty years. Industrial psychologists have certainly played a part in this development. In the first place, their researches into the types of lighting and ventilation that are best for human efficiency have led to bigger and wider windows, to lighter and brighter schoolrooms, and to systems of ventilation that pay as much attention to the physical properties of the air that surrounds the body as to the chemical constitution of the air that enters the lungs. Secondly, their study of such topics as the best height, size, and shape of tables and chairs has had a direct effect on school furniture. Thirdly, their constant emphasis on the general need for designing buildings and equipment in relation to the psychological characteristics of the persons who are to use them has influenced the outlook of architects, engineers, and others who are responsible for the building and equipment of schools. But we must not exaggerate the influence of psychology in this connexion. The great improvement in the physical structure of schools has been mainly the result of advances in hygiene and architecture, on which the influence of psychology has been at best indirect.

Another example of an educational change that owes less to psychology than to other sciences is the greatly increased provision of school meals. Here again psychologists have not been altogether out of the picture. Although many of their researches into the relation between mental and nutritional factors in children have been seriously handicapped by the absence of any clinical or other method that is known to provide a valid assessment of a child's nutritional status, they have at least indicated that while there is a fairly wide range of nutrition on both sides of the normal within which no appreciable difference in mental ability or mental output is found, outside this range inferior mental output is discernible. We may also mention one particular English investigation. Seymour and Whitaker, of the National Institute of Industrial Psychology, measured the progress of two groups of school children, who had been matched for age, intelligence, physical condition, and educational attainment, and were taught in the same classes. The children in the first group were given a meal on arriving at school, while those in the second were not; and it was found that the children in the first group improved ten per cent. more in educational attainment than the others. Psychological experiments of this sort have contributed to the growing awareness that a child's progress in school is affected by his physical condition and the amount that he eats. But it must be admitted that they have formed only a small part of the voluminous scientific work on animal and human nutrition which has lain behind the decision of Parliament that schools shall provide meals and free milk for their pupils.

Turning now to some of the educational changes in which psychology has been, not an incidental, but the predominant influence, we may consider first the new methods of assessing and classifying pupils, particularly the growing use of intelligence tests, attainment tests, and cumulative record cards.

Intelligence tests ultimately derive from the work of Galton in Great Britain and of J. M. Cattell in America. Galton has been called 'the father of mental tests', since it was he who first sought to investigate statistically the inter-relation of mental traits. But it was Cattell who invented the name 'mental test', when he used it in 1896 to describe the psychological tests that he had applied to Columbia students; and intelligence tests, as we now know them, first began to be constructed in the early years of the present century. Their development owes much to Binet in France, and to such psychologists as Terman, Thorndike, and Thurstone in America. But four British psychologists, Ballard, Burt, Spearman, and Thomson, have done at least as much as any others to establish the principles on which such tests must be constructed and standardized, and to demonstrate that there are many theoretical and practical purposes for which they can be profitably employed.

These tests, which are carefully constructed and standardized, assess the capacity for relational and constructive thinking. They are objective in the sense that a candidate's performance obtains the same score by whomever it be marked. They are not, and are not claimed to be, infallible: but they are the best measures of intelligence that we possess. They have greatly facilitated research into such problems as the distribution of intelligence, the growth of intelligence, the influence of heredity on intelligence, the relation between intelligence and physique, and the relation between intelligence and other mental qualities. Thus in the two Scottish Mental Surveys, carried out in 1932 and 1947 by the Scottish Council for Research in Education, an intelligence test was given to all children aged eleven, and analysis of the results has laid bare many interesting and important facts, as, for example, that the more intelligent children come from smaller families. The average score of only children was 42; of children with one sibling, 41·6; with three siblings, 35·3; and with seven siblings, 28·8.

But intelligence tests are not only useful in educational research; they also have direct practical uses in education. First, the Terman-Merrill and similar individual tests have replaced the old crude methods used in the diagnosis of mental deficiency. Secondly, group tests are increasingly used in large primary schools to grade children according to their ability and thus to secure more homogeneous classes, which can each be given suitable lessons and taught at a suitable pace. This is very desirable, because, among children of ten, for example, some 10 per cent. are more intelligent than the average child of twelve, while another 10 per cent. are less intelligent than the average child of eight. In the past, children of widely differing intelligence were often taught in the same class. As a result, the dull were driven to keep up with the bright, and the bright were kept back by the dull. Now, some schools have a fast-moving group for the bright, a slow-moving group for the dull, and an average-moving group for those betwixt and between—which means that each child is getting the sort of instruction that suits him.

Thirdly, a standardized test of intelligence is now an important element in the examinations for entry into secondary schools. In England, for example, 103 of the 106 Local Education Authorities now use intelligence tests in this way. The usual procedure is one that combines a test of intelligence with tests of attainment in English and arithmetic and a report from the child's primary school. The value of including a test of intelligence has been proved by many investigations. Thus Emmett in Yorkshire compared the head teachers' assessments of 765 children at the end of their third year in secondary schools with their scores in an admission examination comprising a group intelligence test, a paper in English, and a paper in arithmetic. He found that the best single measure of later performance was given by the intelligence test, and that 'when the three variables are considered *as a team*, the intelligence test is significantly superior in prognostic value to the English or arithmetic papers; it is, in fact, almost equal to the English and arithmetic papers taken together in their best weighted combination'. Similarly, McClelland in Dundee and McMahon in Cornwall, showed that while an intelligence test might not always be the best single measure of a child's subsequent performance in a secondary school, its presence increased the prognostic value of the entrance examination; and at the recent meeting of the British Association in Newcastle, Peel reported a follow-up investigation in County Durham which showed that the addition of an intelligence test so improved the validity of the initial examination that it enabled the number of misfits to be reduced by a quarter.

Fourthly, intelligence tests are widely used in vocational guidance—in the technique, devised by psychologists, whereby children are assessed and advised as to the occupations in which they are most likely to be successful and happy. Occupational success, of course, depends also on special aptitudes, attainments, physical qualities, interests, and character traits, which must also be taken into account. But there are many occupations in which high intelligence is a prerequisite, though not a guarantee of success. A boy of no more than average intelligence who attempts to train for one of the higher professions is wasting his time. Conversely, where a person of high intelligence is employed on routine work, his talents are lost to the community, and he himself may suffer great unhappiness and frustration. In doubtful cases, an intelligence test may save years of misdirected effort.

The value of intelligence tests in vocational guidance and selection was made plain in the armed forces of the United Kingdom, the British Dominions, and the United States during the Second World War. The navies, armies, and air forces of all these countries included one or more intelligence tests in the procedure by which recruits were selected for different training courses, and in the procedure by which candidates for commissions were assessed. In *Personnel Selection in the British Forces* Vernon and Parry give a full account of the British experience. They show, for example, that when a selection procedure involving intelligence tests was introduced the overall failure rate of mechanics and fitters in the Fleet Air Arm fell from more than one in seven to less than one in twenty; of special operators in the Auxiliary Territorial Service from three in five to one in seven; and of Army tradesmen from one in five to one in nine.

Besides standardized tests of intelligence, standardized tests of educational attainment have also begun to be widely used in schools. They, too, are objective. They consist of a large number of brief questions, instead of a few long ones; and every question is so arranged that all markers agree as to the rightness or wrongness of an answer. Standardized attainment tests are designed to assess knowledge or skill in some general subject, like English or arithmetic, or in some special aspect of such a general subject, like spelling or reading in English and multiplication or decimals in arithmetic.

Attainment tests in English and arithmetic now usually accompany intelligence tests in the selection of pupils for secondary schools. They have replaced the old type of paper in these subjects, and their prognostic value has been established by many inquiries. In general, attainment tests give better predictions of subsequent performance in the secondary school than papers of the more orthodox type, and they increase the validity of entrance examinations in which they are combined with tests of intelligence. They are also useful in determining to what extent, and in what precise ways, an individual child is backward or advanced for his age in the basic subjects. In this connexion the concepts of Reading Age, Arithmetic Age, and others, have been added to that of Mental Age, so that a child of nine, for example, who does as well as the average child of ten in an intelligence test, but only as well as the average child of eight in tests of attainment in reading and arithmetic, is said to possess a mental age of ten, and reading and arithmetic ages of eight. These tests are also often employed in comparing one class or school with another, and in assessing the relative effectiveness of different methods of teaching. Moreover, they have proved valuable not only in education, but in other fields; an attainment test in arithmetic, for example, proved surprisingly successful in predicting proficiency in various courses of training during the war. Indeed, tests of this type are now so firmly established that it is perhaps permissible to refer to the need for their being accompanied by an essay-paper in examinations for admission to secondary schools. Primary-school teachers, like others, are apt to adjust their teaching to the examinations that their pupils must sit. Consequently, if the examination for admission to secondary schools consists entirely of standardized tests, in which the questions are answered merely by an underlining, a tick, a word, or a number, the teaching of English composition in the final year of the primary school inevitably suffers and sometimes disappears altogether. For this reason many psychologists deplore the fact that only 37 of the 106 local education authorities in England now require an essay, or some other form of English composition, in their special-place examinations. They are of the opinion that, however defective an essay may be as a means of assessment or prediction (and it is certainly defective in these respects), it should be retained as an element in the selection of secondary-school pupils, simply in order to preserve the teaching of English in primary schools.

Besides developing intelligence tests, attainment tests—and tests of special aptitudes, which I can only mention in passing —psychologists have also directed their attention to the form in which a child's progress in school should be recorded. They stress the fact that, in assessing a child, whether for educational or vocational guidance, a snapshot technique, which lasts only a few hours, can never be fully satisfactory; and they hold that examinations and objective tests should supplement, not supplant, a cumulative record of the child's development compiled by the teachers who have known and taught him. Consequently, they have investigated the design of school record cards, and the way in which all relevant information can best be expressed. In this connexion they have urged that the cumulative record card should contain as many objective assessments as possible; they have demonstrated the value of rating scales and similar devices for making the subjective judgements of teachers more precise and effective; and they have shown how the setting and marking of ordinary examinations may be improved.

Standardized tests of abilities and attainments, and the new cumulative record cards, have greatly benefited education. But may I say that psychologists are anxious that enthusiastic testers and recorders should always keep three things in mind? First, schools exist for the education, not for the assessment, of children; and examinations, tests, and records are valuable only in so far as they enable the educational and vocational guidance of children to be improved: they are means, not ends. Secondly, many other aspects of a pupil are as important as his abilities and attainments, and among children of normal intelligence even progress in school work is probably affected more by determination or persistence than by anything else. Thirdly, tests and other psychological techniques of assessment, like ordinary examinations, are liable to ineradicable sources of error, though here, as Vernon has said, 'it is fair to claim that British and American psychologists know more about the predictive value and the limitations of their tests and other methods than do any of the hosts of organizations which conduct educational, professional, trade or other examinations'.

A second change that is mainly due to psychological research is the much greater provision that is now made for defective, dull, handicapped, backward, difficult, and otherwise exceptional children.

During the past fifty years special schools have been established for mentally defective children, with the special curricula and special methods of teaching that psychologists like Burt and Kennedy Fraser have shown to be most appropriate. Moreover, special classes in ordinary schools are being increasingly provided for children who, though not below the borderline of mental deficiency, are nevertheless so dull as to be out of place among children of normal intelligence.

Handicapped children, whether their defects be physical or mental, are also much better educated now than they were when Sully was pleading for greater attention to their psychological plight and educational needs. It is now realized that the teacher of the handicapped child must have expert training as well as special sympathies, and a book like Heck's *Education of Exceptional Children* shows the immense amount of research that underlies the new arrangements that have come, or are coming, into force for children who are blind, partially sighted, deaf, crippled, or defective in speech, or who belong to another of the eleven classes of handicapped children for whom provision is envisaged in England.

Backward children are also receiving much more attention. Here Burt's classic work and the equally valuable work of Schonell have been a stimulus and a guide to many teachers and administrators. These psychologists and others have laid bare the intellectual, emotional, and environmental causes of backwardness in spelling, arithmetic, reading, and composition. In backwardness in reading, for example, they have shown among other things the disabling effect of weak perception of complex patterns; the absence of dullness in 40 per cent. of the cases; the importance of 'reading readiness', which is a matter both of eye-movements and of experience; the great influence of emotional factors; and the detrimental effect of poor home-conditions and frequent change of school. They have also investigated the treatment appropriate to backward children; and, apart from detailed advice, Schonell has elaborated seven general principles: (i) individual consideration of the backward child, (ii) thorough diagnosis, (iii) early success for the pupil in the backward subject, (iv) the removal of emotional barriers, (v) a new orientation towards the backward subject through new methods of learning, (vi) frequent, planned remedial lessons, and (vii) co-operation with the parents, particularly in the case of brighter children.

The founding of Child Guidance Clinics has also resulted from the work of psychologists. When Sully founded the British Association for Child Study, no such clinic existed; now there are more than 140 in the United Kingdom. These clinics provide expert guidance for children who exhibit some disorder or difficulty of thought or behaviour which unaided common sense cannot explain and the ordinary methods of correction cannot remove. They are not concerned with the certification or treatment of mental defectives, nor do they deal solely or mainly with delinquents, though they do provide guidance for children who have begun to practise lying, bullying, truancy, stealing, or some other form of misbehaviour. Their primary purpose is to help children, who, while otherwise normal, possess some removable disability or difficulty—like abnormal timidity, morbid anxiety, stammering, or sleep disturbances—which neither time nor punishment can cure. These clinics have arisen out of the early work of Ballard and Burt in Great Britain and of Healy in America, and their organization provides for a thorough psychological and medical examination of each child and for direct contact with his home environment. That they satisfy a need, and that they constitute one of the most important educational changes due to psychology, is shown by the fact that the rapid founding of new clinics hardly keeps pace with the growing number of parents, teachers, doctors, and social agencies, who wish to refer children to them.

Highly gifted children could also benefit from the putting into practice of the results of psychological research into their educational needs. But it must be confessed that, in educational organization and planning, average and handicapped children, for whom it is easier to make an emotional appeal, usually receive more consideration than is given to exceptionally intelligent children. In the United States, it is true, Terman and others have made careful studies of large groups of gifted children over many years, and there is increasing realization of the need for what Heck calls 'a regularly developed programme for finding all specially gifted children, and for giving them the special training required to develop their talents'. And in many of the States, special classes, special 'enrichment courses', (and, though this is objectionable, special schools), are beginning to be provided. But in Great Britain at present the claims of the ablest pupils are perhaps too seldom pressed.

A third educational change that has been mainly due to psychology is the increased emphasis on the importance of activity and interest in learning. Research has firmly established that learning is essentially an active, not a passive, process; that active recall is much more effective than mere passive repetition; that children grasp best what they have not merely assimilated but also expressed or 'done something to, with or about'. For example, Gates long ago showed learning is much more effective when the learning period is partly spent in active recall than when it is wholly devoted to assimilation. And, more recently, Northway has demonstrated that, when children learn material 'by dealing with it in various ways', they can use it in new ways, relate it to other material, and reconstruct it in new forms, much more satisfactorily than when they learn it merely by repetition without being encouraged to ask questions about it or to do anything with it.

It must not be thought, however, that every 'activity method' that can be encountered in schools rests on a sound psychological basis. Some of these methods seem to derive from the view that a child should always be physically active, should never sit quietly at a desk reading a book or learning a Latin declension, and should never be instructed in anything but left to find everything out for himself. Such a view is not supported by psychology, which has found no reason to suppose that children come to harm if they are sometimes sedentary, and every reason to expect that schools will deteriorate if the value of good, systematic instruction and training is minimized. Active recall and constructive thinking are important, but they are futile unless there has been accurate assimilation of the relevant facts and principles, and psychologists have no more desire than other people to see schools turning out self-confident but ill-informed pupils who 'don't know when they don't know'.

The current emphasis on interest also seems to make a word of warning appropriate. It is, of course, true that psychological research has underlined the immense importance of motivation in learning and the fundamental need for adjusting education to the children's interests as well as their abilities; and only a very foolish and inexperienced teacher would fail to take account, in every lesson, of the interests that his pupils possess. But sustained effort is also important. In spite of Mr. Nigel Balchin's plea that all uninteresting work could, and should, be abolished, there are many necessary tasks in school, as in later life, that cannot all the time be intrinsically interesting, and it is an essential part of education that children should learn to carry through a task to the end and not give it up as soon as they find it uncongenial. As William James, one of the founders of modern psychology, said long ago: the philosophy of tenderness in education, the view that interest must be assiduously awakened in everything and all difficulties smoothed away, too often leads to 'lukewarm air, from which the bracing oxygen of effort is left out'.

A fourth educational change on which psychology has had considerable influence is the increasing attention given by primary and secondary schools to their pupils' emotional and social development. Although the typical school in England or Scotland, unlike the typical American school, does not make the 'social efficiency' of its pupils its principal aim, it no longer concentrates on the instruction of the intellect to the neglect of the education of the emotions and social training.

Three groups of social scientists have contributed to this change. First, James in his *Principles*, and McDougall in his *Introduction to Social Psychology*, helped to break down the preoccupation with cognition which characterized British psychology as it was presented by Ward and Stout, and aroused in successive generations of intending teachers a lively interest in motivation, and in instincts, emotions, and sentiments, and their role in the formation of character. Secondly, Freud, Adler, and Jung, in developing psycho-analysis and its derivatives, not only stressed the importance of our conscious and unconscious motives —not only changed the emphasis in psychology from the acquisition of knowledge to the springs of thought and conduct—but also, in the light of clinical evidence, showed the importance of infancy in emotional growth, and argued that the conflicts that cause breakdown in adult life are usually those that revive the unresolved conflicts of childhood. The work of these three psychologists, which now colours the whole contemporary climate of thought, has naturally affected education, where it has led to the provision of nursery schools, to the importance now attached to the child's 'inner security', and to increased recognition of the profound and far-reaching influence of emotional factors on progress in school. Thirdly, the social aspects of education have been brought to the fore by social anthropologists, like Mead and Benedict, whose comparative studies of primitive communities (and, indeed, of the British, the Americans, and the Japanese) have led them to stress the importance of 'culture-patterns', and to suggest that the personality of an individual is mainly a product of the ideals and institutions of the social group to which he belongs. And this emphasis on the social determinants of thought and behaviour has been reinforced by the work of sociologists and social psychologists, like Lewin and his colleagues, whose enthusiasm for 'field-theory' has led them (but not all other psychologists) to regard the individual as little more than an ever-changing 'dynamically structured region' within the total 'field' of social and other forces that are continually acting upon him.

As a result of these influences, the emotional and social aspects of children now loom large in educational literature, and 'self-expression' and 'social adjustment' are only two of the many similar phrases which contemporary students of education encounter again and again. Here, too, I may perhaps be allowed to enter a *caveat*. Let no one suppose that research in child psychology has shown that children are born wholly good, or that they are irreparably harmed if adults curb or correct them, or that nothing matters except their social competence, or that they should be given absolute freedom to do as they like. Certainly a child needs emotional security, and he also needs a sense of achievement and a sense of companionship: these are essentials. But if he is to develop a good, well-organized character; if he is to acquire a reasonable respect for authority, and for the rights and wishes of other people; if he is to make effective use of his powers; if he is to have a stable framework within which he can live and grow up: if any of these desirable results is to be achieved, the child must not be deprived of the controlling and disciplinary influence of parents and teachers. The discipline provided for children must, of course, be consistent and reasonable, not capricious or harsh; and there should be ample opportunity, at home and at school, for children to develop self-reliance, enterprise, and initiative. But in education, as in the rest of life, order is necessary as well as liberty, and all our clinical work with children confirms the common-sense view that the doctrine of absolute freedom, of the 'absolute and autonomous individual', is both false and detrimental. In nineteenth-century education there was often too much emphasis on order and discipline, and undoubtedly some children were overborne and oppressed. Now the pendulum has swung the other way, and there is often too much emphasis on self-expression and freedom, and undoubtedly some children are over-indulged.

Of the other educational changes that owe much to psychology only five can be dealt with, and even these can only be briefly summarized. First, there is the effect on educational theory and practice of research into the question of transfer of training. In 1901 the early experimental work of Thorndike and Woodworth led them to conclude that 'improvement in any single mental function need not improve the ability in functions commonly called by the same name; it may even injure it, since improvement in any single mental function rarely brings about improvement in any other function, for the working of every function-group is conditioned by the nature of the data in each particular case'. This theory, which Thorndike also expressed in the words, 'a change in one mental function alters any other only in so far as the two functions have as factors identical elements', had an immense effect on the construction of curricula in America; it led to the introduction of the 'unit' or 'credit' system, which so many people have found cause to deplore. Later research has confirmed the finding that there is no transfer of improvement from one mental activity to another unless there are usable elements common to the two activities, but it has also shown (*a*) that these common elements need not relate to the objective data or material involved in the activities, but may be elements of method or attitude; and (*b*) that a common element is most usable and effective when the learner becomes clearly conscious of its nature and of its general applicability. Consequently, while the traditional ideas about 'formal training' have never recovered from their conflict with the facts disclosed by Thorndike's research, Thorndike's theory of 'identical elements' must be reinterpreted to cover the cases where a subject in school is so taught as to cause the pupils to acquire methods or ideals which improve their performance in other subjects as well.

Secondly, research into the growth of children's abilities and attainments has led to the provision of more appropriate textbooks for schools. Thus, studies in the growth of vocabulary have led to the preparation of reading-books that take account of the ascertained facts about the words that children of different ages may reasonably be expected to know or to learn. Similarly, studies in spelling have led to the construction of spelling lists which are much better than the old lists, in that they omit words that are too rare to be worth bothering about, or too easy or too difficult for children of the age for which the list is intended.

Thirdly, psychologists are to a large extent responsible for the marked attention now given to the part-time education of young people under 18 whose full-time education has ceased. Stanley Hall's pioneering study of adolescence, the work of Burt and Healy in connexion with juvenile delinquency, and the stream of books and articles on adolescence that have since appeared, have all created a widespread interest in the physical, intellectual, emotional, and social development of the adolescent, and have led to a great change in the quantity and quality of what is called youth work. However, as Wheeler urged at the 1949 Annual Meeting of the British Psychological Society, if the projected county colleges are to be founded on a sounder psychological basis than the three types of secondary school, there is need for 'immediate and careful consideration of the available psychological evidence, and a stepping-up of research on young workers' in order to determine their educational urges and needs. A certain amount of work in this field has already been done; Wheeler referred, for example, to the work of James and Moore, of Wall and of Kitchen. But more is needed; and, as Sir Philip Morris also said at the same meeting, the help of psychologists is particularly necessary in connexion with (*a*) the effects of employment on young people's educational interests, (*b*) the attitudes to county colleges of parents, teachers, employers, and the young people themselves, and (*c*) the organization, curricula, and standards that such colleges should adopt.

Fourthly, psychological investigations into incentives have affected the methods used to induce pupils to make the most of their abilities. Indeed, it may fairly be said that educationists have been much more ready than industrialists to apply the results of this research. They have been quick to consider what is known about the influence on effort and work of (*a*) rewards and penalties, (*b*) praise and blame, (*c*) a definite target, (*d*) knowledge of one's own performance and progress, and of the relation of one's own performance to that of comparable people, (*e*) the social conditions in which the work is done, and (*f*) the superiority of incentives, which, in Mace's phrase, are 'personal, proximate and precise'.

Fifthly, psychological studies and experiments have led to new methods of teaching, which are now not only introduced to intending teachers by institutes of education and teachers' training colleges, but are also being brought to the notice of practising teachers by their various professional organizations. Thus, to take one example, the Aberdeen Branch of the Educational Institute of Scotland, believing that 'the discoveries which scientific investigation has made can lead to more satisfying and more satisfactory work for both pupil and teacher', has recently conducted a series of lectures on what it describes as 'the modern approach' to the teaching of reading, spelling, composition, and arithmetic.

Having now surveyed three types of educational change—changes that have had no scientific background, changes whose scientific background has been mainly non-psychological, and changes that have been greatly influenced by psychology—may I add three concluding remarks? First, although psychology is the systematic study of thought and behaviour in general, not merely of the thought and behaviour of children, the psychologist is always glad when his findings benefit education. And he is equally glad that schools are so willing to provide him with opportunities for making the factual studies and conducting the field experiments that are necessary to the development of his science. Secondly, he has no wish to be, or even to seem, a prophet, priest, and king; he does not pretend to omniscience in human affairs; and, though he is very willing to place information and advice at the disposal of others, he has no wish to direct them, even in the way they should go. Thirdly, when people who value the education that they received in their youth find themselves inclined to regard the present-day school as a disconcerting combination of a crèche, a clinic, a canteen, a carpenter's shop, and a club, will they please make sure, before they blame the psychologist, that the changes they dislike and deplore are not ultimately due to the opinions, forcibly expressed but not scientifically based, of dominant members of an influential Committee?

7

Some fundamental Questions raised by Education's New Role

L. A. REID

MY title is 'Some fundamental questions raised by Education's new role'. I do not propose to try to define the role precisely, but I shall be thinking of it in terms of the various *ideals* which have been so often proclaimed and written down in the last six or seven years (as for example in the *Government White Paper* of 1943), in terms of the structural and other changes brought about by the Act of 1944, and finally as a highly functional idea, as serving English society in its various aspects, personal, social, professional, industrial, political—all in a complex and critical world setting.

It is important that we should not accept any role for education simply as something given, to be taken for granted. Our business in thinking about education—and it is an alarming if exhilarating challenge—is not simply to reflect upon the principles of what education is actually doing, or even what it should be doing if it is to fulfil a given role, but to consider, and to keep considering, as every short page of contemporary history is turned, the role itself. The day-to-day worker in education must, up to a point, accept demands which are made of him by society. But there is a level—and it is the level of what can be called in a wide sense 'philosophy of education'—at which we must stand over and judge, not only what education is doing and how efficient it is in fulfilling the demands society makes of it, but the rightness of those demands. The Government White Paper of 1943 is headed by a quotation, 'Upon the education of the people of this country the fate of this country depends'. This, I take it, should not mean *simply* that it will be the worse for the country if education does not give it what the country demands, but that the fate of the country depends on its demands being the right sort of demands, and that these can only be discovered by education which is both broad and deep.

Let us then consider one or two of the 'fundamental questions' which are raised by education's new role.

The word 'fundamental' is important. It is difficult not to develop a certain myopia when one is engaged in the tasks of everyday education, whether in teaching or in administration. Nor is it easy to keep perspective even if one is thinking of education in quite broad ways, as is the purpose of these lectures. To conceive of education in relation to the State, for example, *may* be to be tempted to identify education with training in citizenship, and to forget the important fields of personal development and social but non-political relationships. Even when, in this context of political citizenship, we speak quite sincerely of religion (as did the Conservative *Report* of 1942 on Education (*Looking Ahead*)) we are apt to discover ourselves supporting religious education because religion is 'so important for national survival', because without sound religion a State may become corrupt and decay. In other words we are tempted to forget the proper autonomy of religion. Or if we are thinking of education for industrial society, it is not difficult to lose sight of wider human needs. And, if our habit is to conceive of education in sociological (or psychological) terms, there is a danger of becoming too deterministic, or of conceiving persons or groups simply as instances of generalizations, perhaps to be controlled or manipulated or directed according to what the sociologist (or psychologist) may assume, without thinking much about it, to be good. Or, again, desirable as is the application of scientific method to education, there is a danger, in so analysing, of becoming so intoxicated by the pleasure of the game of scientific analysis and verification that something, living individual human beings or social groups with their individual *ethos*, slips through the analytic meshes. Intellectual vested interests easily spring up, and with them fragmentation and distortion of the whole truth.

But beyond all this, and whatever we are doing and thinking in education, there are assumptions and presuppositions of a very fundamental kind which make and shape and direct our ideas. It is dangerous to assume that because they are largely hidden they do not matter, or that we in England are really agreed about all essentials. Humanitarian in the main we certainly are: 'Western values' we certainly share: but underneath there are dividing philosophies of human nature—philosophies which if consistently developed can affect both the theory and the practice of education more than is commonly recognized.

The divisions are, no doubt, various and subtle, not to be expressed in terms of a single and too simple line-up. But for the sake of brevity and point I will give as an instance one of the central and fundamental issues of our mental and spiritual life to-day, indicating its bearing upon educational thought and practice.

I mean the issue between what is called scientific humanism and Christianity. Scientific humanism, as an explicit worked-out philosophy, may be the product of a few of the intellectuals and is sponsored in various forms by Russell, Huxley, Bernal, Waddington, Hogben, Alex Comfort, Erich Fromm, and others. But its assumptions permeate widely, and it is certainly the unconscious philosophy of many a young graduate originating from the science sixth.

For scientific humanism, man and his mind are wholly a product of natural evolution; there is no supreme creative mind which made him. Human mind and human nature are the highest things we know: scientific humanism is *humanism* because humanity is the final object of its concern, and the human mind the sole creative source, not only of the 'improvement of man's estate', but of man himself. And it is *scientific* humanism because it is by knowledge, and chiefly by scientific knowledge, that the improvement will take place. By the physical, medical, psychological, sociological sciences, developed and applied, we may hope—if disaster does not overtake us first—to make a loftier race and a finer world. For scientific humanism, human values are purely human products and a purely human concern. Man,

in Erich Fromm's phrase, is 'for himself': there is no one else
he can be for. Man is the measure of all things. And as he was
born yesterday, to-morrow will be his end. The days of man are
—ultimately, and not in appearance only—as grass: his life is a
brief flowering: the wind passeth over it and it is gone, and the
place thereof shall know it no more. And, for the humanist,
there is no 'Mercy of the Lord from everlasting to everlasting'.
That is the language of wishful thinking.

Dr. Alex Comfort, in a recent broadcast, has put it well.

Throughout the whole religious tradition, we can see endless traces
of man, but nothing which is an unequivocal token of mind or of
standards apart from the mind and standards of man.

And it seems to me that, relying on the evidence, we can see no
signs of moral purpose or of standards anywhere save in man. The
most vivid impression which we get from the study of the universe is
not that a God created man, but that man has created God.

The more fully we study the human mind, the more we learn
about the pattern of its desires and fears, the more like our own
voice does this voice from the universe become. The more irresistible
is the conclusion that it *is* the echo of our own voice. Man looks into
the universe for God, and finds his own patterns of order and reason.
He looks into the natural order for the righteousness of God and finds
his own ethical values, his own conceptions of beauty and truth. He
listens for the voice of God, and hears his own voice answer him. And
when he confronts the tradition of his ancestors with their conviction
of a purpose and a will underlying the scheme of reality, he finds his
own purpose and will. The God of his tradition is a mirror in which
he sees himself.

As against this, the Christian answer is—or was until recently
—familiar. Or, at least, the sounds of its words are, even now,
not altogether unknown to a new generation, though its meaning is less understood, popularly and by the intelligentsia, than
almost ever before. For Christianity, man is not *finally* a product
of nature and the highest of all beings, but is created by God.
Truly human values are not *finally* of human origin or in human
hands: man is not 'for himself'. His chief good, his chief End, is
to 'glorify God and enjoy Him for ever'. Increased knowledge
and human betterment are important and are enjoined, but

man achieves fullness of being not *finally* by his own unaided effort and knowledge, but only through complete self-surrender to God. The creative love which is needed to transform the world and man's nature cannot be created finally in the human heart but derives from the divine love. And the final setting of man's life is not the 'three score years and ten' of the psalmist, but eternity.

I must apologize for taking time even to outline this now familiar contrast. My concern here is not exposition or defence or evaluation—though I ought to say that my own allegiance is to the Christian side. But I am concerned to indicate, if only briefly, that this typical contemporary opposition is of direct relevance to education, that, wherever the truth may lie, what we hold makes a great *difference* to our theory and practice of education, and that—whether it be for better or worse—English education cannot be nearly as 'Christian' as commonly supposed.

There will be great differences, for example, about *moral* education. If, as Dr. Comfort says, 'there are no signs of moral purpose or of standards anywhere save in man', moral *authority* will emanate finally from somewhere in the human sphere. For Christianity, on the other hand, the moral order, established by God, is intrinsic to the universe. For humanism—and this becomes important at a time of the dissolution of whole societies —there must necessarily be a feeling of moral evanescence.

I do not mean at all that the moral fibre of the good humanist is weak. On the contrary he exhibits a noble stoicism emphasizing self-reliance and self-composure—though he tempers this and modern stoicism by speaking of *control* of nature. Dr. Comfort expresses it finely in the same series of broadcasts. He says:

I think we can guess at the features of the portraits of the future, the portraits which have yet to be painted and hung. They are the faces of men who are experiencing the strains of facing the discoveries which they have made. They are faces looking into a universe from which they expect neither quarter nor co-operation, a universe in which their standards and values, the standards and values of humanity, the material of the tradition of religion and tradition of science, have no part. They are the faces of individuals who, so far as they can ascertain, have no immortal future into which to look forward, and whose whole existence as a race, as well as individuals, could be ended by a change of a few degrees in the temperature of the earth's surface. Bertrand Russell has said that they look forward 'from the firm foundation of unyielding despair'. I would not use that word despair. Like Macbeth, they can despair their charm against fate, but in doing so I think they grow to a fuller stature. Their future is in their own hands. The very discoveries which have destroyed their illusions have given them the means of controlling, and possibly mastering, the environment which has produced them.

These are noble sentiments, consistent with the humanist philosophy. But noble or not, this Stoic 'assent', combined with strong self-assertiveness and, at least, a 'non-ultimate' hope, is totally *different* from the nobility of the best Christian sentiments, the Christian 'assent', the Christian strength through dependence, through 'waiting upon the Lord'. And the whole approach to moral education, by those who believe in the one or in the other and its orientation, will be different.

Again, the two views will involve different teachings about the attitude of children, and all of us, to nature. If what Dr. Comfort says is true, that 'man looks into the universe for God, and finds his own patterns of order and reason', then surely it will be irrational and unscientific to teach children a reverence for nature? Delight, wonder, curiosity, excitement—yes. But if we are to be rational, hardly reverence. If they tend to feel anything of the sentiment of the creature-creator relationship when they learn of the wonders of the human body, or the stars in their courses, or the structure of a flower, they must be encouraged to grow out of that immaturity. Christianity, on the other hand, does teach reverence for the created thing.

And what of our attitude to children, and the tone of our teaching of them? They must be greatly different in the two cases of scientific humanism and Christianity. Disciples of either view may, of course, love and care for children, perhaps greatly. But for the scientific humanist the morning life of the child, like the life of man, is evanescent, the beauty of a moment which will have passed a moment hence. Life is like the poppy: 'You seize the flower, the bloom is shed'. For the Christian, on the other hand, the life and joys of children are 'bright shoots of everlastingness'. How can these different beliefs fail, in the long run, to affect, in their different ways, the school or home atmosphere?

I do not say that the differences I have cited are usually affirmed or recognized, or that beliefs are carried to their logical conclusion. I am arguing only that they do exist, that beliefs and attitudes are changing, and that we should be aware of their influence in education.

There is, of course, a lot more to be said—and to be done—than this. If there are these fundamental differences, it is true too that we have to live together in tolerance, peace, and co-operation as far as we can, and without sacrifice of principle. The spirit, methods, and conditions of that co-operation are hard to seek and a large problem requiring separate investigation. Let us note it and pass on.

Another fundamental question, not unconnected with what has been said, is, 'Who shall control the direction of education?'

Sir Fred Clarke, in his recent address to the British Association, stressed the idea that education is 'a main agency of social control'. But who or what is to control this control? *Quis custodiet* . . . ? In the past, education was largely a matter of tradition. But with nineteenth-century liberalism came scientific study and 'the search for *rational* aims and principles, in the guidance of practice against the dictates of tradition; so we get that application of biological and psychological studies to the understanding of education, which has been so fruitful and in many ways so beneficial'.

Certainly it has been extraordinarily fruitful and beneficial. But it has its dangers too. Each of the sciences is a specialism which for its own purposes must abstract from the concreteness of things so that we may tend to lose sense of its wholeness, substituting expert judgement for sensitive searching experience. It would certainly be dangerous to look for guidance and control of education in any one single direction. Biology, psychology, sociology, do all greatly help us to understand education and its proper content and method, yet none singly but is an unsure guide. Neither can we simply sum their results. On the other hand, tradition is obviously not enough, nor contemporary popular opinion. And no government in itself possesses the wisdom: indeed, for a government as a government to decide for itself what education shall be is to us here in England an utterly loathsome idea.

What we do need is to draw upon all these resources—and, most of all, perhaps, to draw upon the richness of our robust empirical knowledge—and to draw upon them with *wisdom*. And I want to argue—it is another form of my first main contention—that philosophy has an important contribution to make to that wisdom. Please do not misunderstand me. I am not saying to the philosophers 'Ye are the people and wisdom shall die with you'. I am certainly not advocating that we should relegate the question of what education ought to be to the professional philosophers as we now understand the word. Yet, as I suggested earlier, much more 'philosophical' thinking is required, and it is, particularly in an era of changing values, a quite indispensable element in any wise judgement of education. For, as has been suggested, we must see the different abstractions in their relationship, we must be aware of the things that are taken for granted, and we must relate all these to the most fundamental thinking about the doctrine of man and his world. If we are content with anything less, education will either be half-blind, empirical only, traditional only (and very uncertainly traditional in an unsettled age), or it will fall a victim in turn to this particularity or that. On the other hand, if we apply philosophy properly, we are being, I think, as 'rational' as we know how to be. Informed, wise, educated opinion, employing the sciences, leavened by philosophy—this should be the final (though fallible) 'custodian' of education.

This has some practical implications. Philosophical education is needed, and is appallingly lacking in educated—in University-educated—people. I do not know whether the average English (as opposed to the Scots) graduate is the most philosophically philistine person in the world, but he is pretty bad. For reasons too large to enter upon here philosophy (outside

Oxford and Cambridge at any rate) has been an academic Cinderella. One cause is perhaps that university teachers, who determine academic policy, are graduates and only a minority of university graduates even know what philosophy is. (The 'philosopher' they tend to regard as something rather like the 'professor' in the detective story.) It is, therefore, difficult to get recognition of its place in a university—since if a person has no philosophy in him there are no arguments which will convince him of its value. And those who have some philosophy do not need arguments.

As a result, English educational thought has been starved—with some exceptions—of its philosophical due. I am sure that this is now beginning to be realized. The University of London took the initiative in establishing a Chair of Philosophy of Education a few years ago and there are stirrings elsewhere. There is a feeling here and there in the training colleges that a more philosophical approach is needed, and I have met teachers and lecturers from all over the country who have strong views about this. But the trouble is that philosophical thinking needs basic and systematic training, and with all the goodwill in the world there are not at present enough trained people. This takes us back to the universities. I hope the time will soon come when some philosophy (hitherto avoided because it is not a 'teaching' subject) will be regarded as an indispensable part of the aspiring educationist. But if so, university departments of philosophy may have to reconsider their policy. A few intending educationists may adopt the 'unpractical' course of taking honours in philosophy, but this, I think, is not what is chiefly required. What is needed are good courses for non-specialists, giving an introductory training in philosophical method and approach. And as it is important that the more general student should recognize that philosophy is a living way of approaching living problems it might in some cases be better to substitute courses which deal philosophically with those issues that are felt to be important by all intelligent students than to offer them the conventional course in history of philosophy. This is, of course, a difficult and debatable question. I am certainly not running down the traditional courses, and I have no wish to dogmatize. Anyhow, there is an important and practical problem here: it is most lamentable that so few teachers and educators are in any way trained to think in an educated way about the principles of what they are doing day by day.

The contention that a great present need of education is well-proportioned wisdom leavened by philosophy, a constant thinking of the relation of immediate needs to basic ones, has a large number of applications. I can only mention briefly one or two of these.

We ought to scrutinize, as has been hinted, the current emphasis upon the *social* function of education. Admittedly, it is quite wrong to conceive of education as an absolute, separated off from history and contemporary needs. It is also healthy to be empirical, as has been our tradition in this country. And we may assent to the quotation from Dr. Huxley, made in Professor Lester Smith's charming little book on *Education in Great Britain*, 'that education, having escaped from religious direction and classical bias so as to become directionless, will require a new slant in the shape of a social direction, and correlated with this will be a change in the status of the whole educational system'. Certainly this is true, but certainly, also, sociological empiricism is not the last word. We have a tendency to believe in the myth of the natural goodness, if left to develop. Not so much of individual man but of an abstraction called society. Society is the measure of all things. Emphasizing the relative, we over-look the universal elements in human nature, we suppose that the universal is a philosopher's invention, a fiction, that has no bearing upon present realities. But the relative and the universal are not exclusive contradictories. Man has a nature—whether he be black or white, whether he lives in a capitalist or socialist society; there is something which is human nature and the philosophers have not been just dreaming when they have striven to conceive of a properly human good, good for all men, as men, though good always in particular ways, and in parti-cular historical situations. Such language is extremely unfashion-able: that it should be so is a good reason for keeping a level head about contemporary fashions. Immediate needs, certainly, are urgent, but it is a form of materialism to neglect to think them together with more general claims.

We must, as I have hinted, scrutinize our moral education too, and also some of the philosophical ethics which may affect it. The aims and methods of moral education will always be determined in the end, I suggested, by what we really believe or assume about the nature of man and the universe in which he lives. Professor Woodward has warned us that we may forget 'that the tragic interpretation of history is still valid'. We may ask, is a simple 'social' theory of ethics adequate when standards are disappearing and whole societies are melting or being blasted away in a night? When they saw the secure world vanishing before their eyes the ancient Stoics had to construct a new ethic in place of Aristotle's excellent but parochial one. Is the modern stoicism—stoicism with a difference—of scientific humanism the true and sufficient answer? Or is the current subjectivism, which pervades a good deal of contemporary philosophical ethics, adequate, not to a fairly comfortable bourgeois existence where one can speculate from a safe base without doing much harm, but to crisis and disaster? Where are we to look for the moral power to say, 'Here stand I; I can do no other'? Or may it, if society and the individual life is threatened, be even worth saying?

We must scrutinize, too, the logic of popular ethical relativism, the loose inference that because duty is always relative to the circumstances (Aristotle has said it all), and that because one's duty shifts therefore there is no duty, and duty has no common nature. And we ought to be sceptical when told that because anthropology shows the extreme variability of beliefs about standards, there cannot be *any* fixed moral principles and no proper human good. Once again it may not, in a settled world, do great harm to throw out these crude concatenations of ideas as though they were intelligent. But if they take root in attitudes, and crisis comes, then may come again the accusation 'the treason of the clerisy'.

We need also to think fundamentally about the content of

education. Given time, there is a lot that might be said about the curriculum. I can only mention it and leave it.

Everyone knows that actual curricula contain subjects which may or may not quite justifiably be there, but which it would puzzle practising teachers to justify. And various pressures, effective but unreasoned, are always operating for eliminations or additions to the curriculum. What is needed here is a careful objective analysis of functions. Dr. Eric James, in his interesting book on *The Content of Education*, has mentioned, for instance, the functions of information, skills, and spiritual development. We have to attempt a comparative evaluation of the various claims and related and systematic thinking about them all. But such evaluation and thinking must always have a basis, as before, in quite fundamental beliefs about what things are most important for the life of human beings. These must, I should say, include social values, but we cannot end up with them. And what we do think and judge about the balance of the curriculum will vary according to whether we are scientific-humanists, Platonists, or Christians. The study of the contents of the curriculum is a philosophical question.

The problem of its unity, and the unity of knowledge, is far larger. Specialism we must have; fragmentation we are getting, because the technical insides of well-fenced subjects are studied by technical bits of persons, and persons self-isolated, instead of subjects being conceived as foci of stretching and multi-coloured areas apprehended by whole living persons, open to one another, with all their faculties alive. No one to-day can take all knowledge to be his province, but the fragmentation of knowledge is parallel to and both cause and effect of not only the fragmentation of personality, but the fragmentation of society. Dr. G. B. Jeffery, in his 1949 Eddington Lecture at Cambridge, has spoken eloquently of the kind of sense of unity of knowledge which was possible in a Cambridge college in the old days—in contrast to the departmental academic living of to-day. To be aware of a specialism as a focal field, a growing point to whose extent there is no limit short of the whole of knowledge, is to do something much more than to construct a schema of integrated concepts—though I am not depreciating that. It is to live in community, and, more, to live in sympathy, humility, sensitiveness, friendship, and, I would say, love, in a society of friends, each growing, each fertilizing the minds and being of the others. I do not think that we fully realize the effect, even upon sheer understanding of the size of knowledge, of the importance of being whole persons and of the education through personal humility and the mutual respect of persons. It is, of course, practically realized here and there, in some good schools, in some colleges, in some other communities where people think and work and create and know one another, and by knowing, learn and grow. But we have not faced the significance of this in education generally at all. There is a fundamental human problem how to live in a knowledge-seeking community as a whole human being, and it is, I believe, in that direction that we must seek for such integration of knowledge as we can attain to, rather than, finally, in schemas of integrated study, important as those undoubtedly are. If only we could do something of this kind to our rising teachers, how much could they not do in turn to those whom they teach and with whom they should be living?

Lastly, we must search not only our minds, but our hearts, about a conception which perhaps affects the general pattern and structure of education rather than its content. I mean the idea of equality.

Our ideas and feelings about equality are full of intellectual confusion and emotional blindness. We have strong sentiments on the subject coming from historical, social, economic, and personal sources, as well as from deep and sound general moral sentiments. It is because our moral sentiments often get mixed up with unclear ideas and doubtful motives that we may find ourselves arguing and advocating, in this direction or that, courses of action which are incompatible both with our more rational judgements and our real moral sentiments. In the next few pages I shall be obliged to say some very general things about equality: I shall not have the space to apply them to individual cases. But I shall be thinking of such controversial questions as: the greater equalization of holidays in different types of schools, the question of salaries of graduate and non-graduate teachers, the symbolism (not merely the descriptive words involved) of parts of the present controversy about the common title for the initial training qualification of all teachers. Again there are questions of the motives for the regulation about the age of leaving-examinations, the arguments for and against comprehensive and multilateral schools, questions about the public schools, about admission to universities. And so on.

There is a positive question, and a normative question. Even these occasionally get mixed up. It ought to be clear that human beings *are*, *in fact*, not equal—indeed, that inequality is universal and no one is equal to anyone else. Yet there is emotional resistance occasionally to the recognition of even this plain fact. I have known some extra-mural students get rather hot about the curve of normal distribution: they did not like to think that people are so unequal, or they wanted to argue, perhaps, that if they are unequal it is really somebody's fault. If x is more intelligent than y, then it *must* be because y has not had a chance. Improve social conditions and all will be fair. People *ought* to be equal. I am not sure whether in their heart of hearts, and putting it parabolically, some people would not like everyone to be just exactly 5ft. 10½ in. in height! There is a great confusion of inequality with injustice.

There *is*, I think, a factual basis for saying that all men are equal, and I personally think it is the proper ground of all normative statements about equality. But it is a factual basis of which—in my opinion—only a religious philosophy can give a coherent account. It is 'factual' not in the ordinary scientific value-separated sense, but in a more ultimate sense in which value and fact are not dichotomized, but in essence united. It is the fact which Christians affirm in a statement of faith when they say that the God of Love created all men as persons, that every person, his life and his destiny, is infinitely precious, and that the prime human obligation of every created person is to love (of course in a defined sense) every other person as a child of God. Every created person in this sense has an equal, divinely given 'right' (for Christians all 'rights' are gifts) to be respected. And the consideration of all a person's human needs (for education and other things) must be in relation to his divinely given vocation.

I have never been able to see how any secular humanism or, indeed, any view of life which is not religious in some such sense as I have described, can show any factual basis for equality. It is of no use saying that all men are to be equally respected as 'rational' beings, because so many are so irrational. And it is of no use to say that all men are to be respected as 'potentially' rational either. *Why*—on any rational grounds other than the religious, or that the patience of God chastens my impulsive fury—should I 'respect' a Nazi thug the 'probability' of whose more rational behaviour may, humanly and scientifically speaking, be just *nil*?

But although there does not seem, as far as I can see, to be any non-religious-rational, scientific or humanistic basis of fact to show that all men *are* in some sense equal, it is, of course, an integral part of the finest Western tradition to believe that in *some* sense they *ought* to be treated equally. The Christian's derivation of this, from his affirmative religion, is clear, and it is likely that the scientific humanist assumes Christian reasoning —if inconsistently—more than he is aware. If, however, he explicitly repudiates it, then he must fall back on a purely normative statement. All men ought—in some sense—to be treated equally. Either this is a dogma or an unexplained postulate, or perhaps it may be said that society has found that behaviour in accordance with this principle works best.

But granted that we assent to the proposition that all men ought, in some sense, to be treated equally—in what sense?

Can we not agree that everyone is—as far as possible—to be given an 'equal' or 'fair' chance of developing his capacities so that he has the opportunities of becoming the best sort of person he can be, both as an individual and as a member of society? The humanist will differ from the Christian in his interpretation of this, the former making final the role of the individual-in-society. The Christian will include this, but will recognize personal obligations which transcend those of society and which may, on occasion, conflict with them. For example, a Christian might justify a long and expensive specialized—*very* 'unequal'—education for a religious vocation which his humanist colleague might possibly grudge as an unfair privilege.

But, leaving these differences, it must be clear that this principle of normative 'equality' entails, without irrationality, *inequality* of nearly every kind. This point can need no argument here. For the greatest total good, however conceived, for the sake of equality in the sense defined, and because in fact different persons' capacities and gifts are so different, there must be the greatest inequalities of opportunity, in, for instance, education. 'Equality of opportunity', so valid in one sense, directly implies inequality of opportunity in another; and educated people mostly recognize this. No informed person holds that because 'all men should be equal therefore everyone has a right to a university education'. And yet—though it is an extreme case—there are ignorant and uninformed people who, in fact, look at the privileges of the undergraduate with a jealous eye. 'Why not my child. . . . ?'

I said that this subject is biased by emotional and intellectual confusion. It always has been so. Sixty years ago the privileged 'unequal' were using all the religious and moral arguments to preserve unchanged their status of inequality. They were defending the divisions of the classes as they were then. And similar spurious, if not blasphemous, arguments are occasionally heard to-day. The Afrikaans Studentebond is reported to have affirmed that 'the difference between the white and coloured sections of the population is an acknowledged fact, and, therefore, created by God'. There exists between the European and non-European 'not a human difference, but a divine one'.

Now, the pendulum having swung, social and emotional prejudices about equality are sometimes given a rational disguise. I am entirely on the side of the social revolution, and I do fully appreciate the justified desire for greater equality. But it would be disingenuous to pretend that whilst in the past all motives were tainted, now all motives are pure. The whole question should be objectively—and sensitively—apprehended, for there is a danger that in a passion for a shallowly conceived equalitarianism precious things may be lost, that black injustice may be done to exceptional and gifted people because the educational 'privileges' they require are not supposed to fit in with 'democratic' equality; and there is the danger that democratic society, instead of being served by the richness of developed differences, will die of the inanition of mediocrity.

Mixed up with the most unexceptionable desires for real and necessary reform there is sometimes envy, jealousy, greed, and spite. There is a desire to drag down and make level because we lack humility and because we hate the undemocratic posture of looking up, or because we cannot rightly look down (as any person in a commanding or responsible position must) without feeling sinfully and damnably superior. And there is the rather odd and muddled, but very prevalent belief that we cannot be good friends unless we are all 'the same'. The fact that a good phrase like 'my station and its duties'—admittedly often abused —will evoke cries of contempt, is a sign that we need not only intellectual but moral purification. And in this reform it is necessary to be aware of emotional poisons working in us. No one can claim a clear conscience here. We all have vested interests. If we are privileged we tend to one-sided inequalitarianism, we tend to defend privilege for the wrong reasons. If we are unprivileged (or even if by social sympathy we have identified ourselves too uncritically with the unprivileged) equally may self-assertion—rather than the motive of service to man and God—tend to bias us. These motives, on both sides, are understandable, and, let us hope, forgivable, especially the motives of the underprivileged. (They had better be forgivable —or we are all quite certainly damned.)

I cannot deal with the application of these ideas to education; indeed, the application is complex and controversial. (But application is the important thing.) All I suggest is that we have to scrutinize our ideas and our consciences far more often than we do, about what things are to be done properly, and what things are not to be done, in the name of equality.

Here I must stop rather than end. For, indeed, there is no end. If I have been at all right, the fundamental questions, being root-questions, have something to do with the colour and shape and vitality and health of every little leaf, twig, and flower of the tree. And as these are infinite, so are the questions infinite.

Yes, the tree is one. May we see it so. It goes on growing lustily. So, let us hope, may we.

8

Constructive Change in Education. A Synthesis

C. H. DOBINSON

THIS chapter attempts three things. Firstly, it seeks to bring together related lines of thought from the preceding pages and to show the quite remarkable degree of assent among the writers. Secondly, it endeavours to concentrate attention upon points in the field of education where early action is desirable. Thirdly, with much temerity, it ventures to suggest what form some of this action might take. It thus proceeds from the general to the particular and substitutes immediate and limited objectives for the broad sweep and the wide vision. But as the interest in a large map of a campaign is only rendered real by the sanguinary advances at small points on the battle front, so in education progress can only be made by effort applied now here, now there, where change is most urgent. Besides, the reader who has been stimulated thus far will probably wish to consider where and in what form his own action and expression of opinion should be made.

It is from the highly placed vantage-point above the din of battle and with a sense of somewhat objective detachment that Mr. C. R. Morris surveys our present educational configuration. 'What are some of the objectives of the 1944 Education Act' he asks, and then 'how far do our educational traditions and accumulated experience make us competent to achieve these purposes?' In a wide survey he considers the changes that have taken place during the last one hundred years and shows how these may be regarded as natural and proper growths in harmony with our national traditions and the fundamentals of our way of life. He regards the three stages at which full-time non-vocational study will end, namely graduation, completion of a grammar-school course and reaching the age of sixteen as being soundly based on our accumulated experience. He emphasizes that after the age of sixteen many pupils can only benefit from further study if they are permitted, for their main activity, to 'go to work' and learn to ply their trades. He suggests that, in comparison with systems of education elsewhere, we are at least holding our own and that an intense degree of self-castigation never has been and never will be productive of heroic virtue. The lines along which we are extending are, he feels, soundly based and, moreover, were accepted with purely minor divergencies of emphasis by all the political parties. In short, we have reason to be confident that whatever further economic stress may await our country, progress and development along the lines already laid down will continue. There is a further reason for this which has not been mentioned, but which, unpleasant though it is, needs to be stated lest the sin of hypocrisy sometimes imputed to our nation creep over us. In a lecture given at the Sorbonne in 1946 Professor C. M. Bowra said: 'It would hardly be unfair to say that most countries have improved their educational methods because they are afraid that if they do not do so they will lose in the competitive struggle against other countries.'

Not only in the field of economics, but in that of the organized destruction which we call modern warfare the same is true. It has been claimed that it was the development of the grammar schools under the 1902 Education Act which saved Britain in the recent war. For it was from these schools that great numbers of the young men came forward with an adequate knowledge of mathematics and science to navigate our aircraft and to officer our scientific warfare. That such things should be counted among the fruits of education is a lamentable reflection upon our age. Yet face such thoughts we must. Nor can we remain unaffected by the number of graduates produced each year in the U.S.S.R.—probably well in excess of one hundred thousand —knowing as we do that the majority of these men and women are servants of the new technology rather than contemplative spirits researching in the realms of philosophy or aesthetic experience.

Similarly the development in the U.S.A. of what is called semi-professional education requiring two years of American college preparation is another educational change which we cannot ignore. This form of education, which will be given more and more in day community colleges, seeks to increase the contribution of each highly qualified professional man or woman by providing him or her with two or three skilled assistants. These will have received not only technical preparation but good general education showing itself in personal development and widened horizons. A notable field for such semi-professional workers is that of medicine and we in this island are not free from problems in this department of our social life.

But as a people we have a natural and a proper reluctance to see education as a process directed mainly to serving the purposes of the community whether in technology or in any other way. We reject not only the claims of all forms of technical experts such as economists to rule us, but we reject also the conception of an education aimed at the production of philosopher kings.

Though less Christian, so far as verbal confession goes, than our Victorian forbears, we are determined that the equality of man in the sight of God shall be followed by the corollary of equality of opportunity in the sight of man. Not only, by the Education Act of 1944, is the spiritual, moral, mental, and physical development of the community now a responsibility of the local education authority, but also the education provided must suit the different ages, abilities, and aptitudes.

As Professor Knight points out, one of the greatest changes in education in this country to-day is the remarkable provision for the education not only of the educationally sub-normal, but of the deaf, the blind, the weakly, and the emotionally disturbed. One should remark, in parenthesis, that similar great developments have been made in education in other countries including the U.S.S.R. where Institutes of Defectology, as they are called, are attached to some of the universities.

In this country, too, there is a further aim implicit in the Education Act of 1944, but finding explicit expression outside the Act in the words 'parity of esteem'. This phrase was coined for application to the three types of secondary school, types which, as Professor Knight reminds us, have never been justified by psychology so far as their application to children at the age of eleven years is concerned. The objective beyond the phrase 'parity of esteem' is that of dissolving, as far as may be possible in an efficient community, all class barriers which separate man from man, restrict his vision, and harden the arteries of compassion. If one of the purposes of education be, as has been claimed, to make men free, then this destruction of class and other barriers within the life of a nation is part of such purpose.

There is, however, a danger that the means adopted to achieve a given end, especially when that end is a change in so delicate a fabric as society, may not only fail to achieve their purpose, but may frustrate it. Mr. Morris has said 'It will be fatal to democracy if we are afraid of quality', and Professor Reid writing of equality 'There is a desire to drag down and make level because we lack humility. . . . And there is the rather odd and muddled, but very prevalent belief, that we cannot be good friends unless we are all "the same".' Professor Kandel turns our attention to those efforts which seek to resolve what one might call the 'trilemma' of grammar school, technical school, and secondary modern school, by the creation of multilateral schools. These are in effect the British counterpart of the American comprehensive high school. The substance of Professor Kandel's charge is that those who wish to fasten this system upon England should first of all have made an objective study of such schools in the U.S.A. and sought to discover whether the physical propinquity of pupils of very different intellectual endowment does in fact produce sympathy, understanding, and goodwill, and lay the foundations of a classless society. From his wealth of experience he claims that no such results accrue. Instead he refers us to carefully garnered evidence that such omnibus schools set up new internal tensions and reflect within the life of the school some of the worst social intolerances found outside. If, as many of the leading minds in the U.S.A. to-day consider, the comprehensive high school has failed to deliver the social goods for which it was created, and, incidentally has resulted in a standard of intellectual achievement which is much lower than that achieved by pupils of the same age in Europe, then, wherever such schools are planned in England we must urge those concerned to think again. In England, says Mr. Morris, a well-tried institution is not hastily scrapped and a well-tried policy not abandoned without a careful review of its successes in the past and the presumed reasons for them. The whole matter is one of profound importance to this country, for if there be one characteristic of English education which most teachers from abroad admire, and wish to copy, it is the effect which school life in England has upon the character and personality of the pupil.

There are several factors responsible for this; one is the relative smallness of our schools. Until comparatively recently we have had very few schools containing more than 600 pupils, and there has been a tradition that the head of the school should set out to know personally every pupil and to have some contact with his parents. In boarding schools this personal contact between teachers and pupils is carried farther by housemaster and tutors. Everywhere there has been the assumption that the headmaster is more than an administrator and that no system of delegation of powers to his subordinates absolves him from ultimate responsibility for every pupil. Though this system puts a heavy burden on the heads, yet it is one which the majority of them readily assume. It calls forth a concern for most aspects of a pupil's life and creates throughout the school a predominant interest in persons rather than in subjects, in human qualities rather than mere intellectual exercise. 'All education which is worthy of the name', says Martin Buber, 'is essentially education of character.' Education, states Mr. Wolfenden, is essentially the influence of one person upon another. If anyone wishes to see a form of schooling in which such influence is at a minimum and in which education of character plays little or no part, let him spend a day in one of the great *lycées* of Paris. Here he will find some 1,500 or 2,000 pupils—a number comparable with that proposed for London's comprehensive schools—and all the machinery of administration necessary to deal with such hordes.

The *professeurs* are specialists—highly qualified men and women desperately keen on their subject and extremely scholarly. They give their lectures in the various class-rooms and then walk out of the building. There are very few of their pupils whom they really know, and some of their colleagues they may never have met. The *proviseur* is a mere administrator, his personality has no proper channel for expression: his office staff is large, the routine well established, and one is tempted to think that his absence would have less effect upon the school than that of any other member of the staff. This is doubtless an exaggeration, but it is the *impression* which one receives because all individuality seems lost in this great factory for the production of examination fodder.

No one supposes that those who plan our great multilateral schools of 2,000 are not aware of these dangers. There will be all sorts of schemes of decentralization and delegation to provide personal contacts with the pupils, but it is difficult to believe that any ingenuity can outwit the force of numbers and prevent the destruction of some of the most valuable features of English education. I should be less insistent on this point were the large multilateral schools the only possible method of moving towards that distant star 'parity of esteem'. The school campus scheme, adopted by many authorities in their plans, seems eminently preferable. Under this arrangement the three types of school will be situated on the same site, sharing the same playing-fields and swimming-bath and with equal physical amenities of every kind. The schools will be able to co-operate in many activities, sporting and cultural, but each school will be small enough to preserve what has been the English tradition in secondary-school life. This includes, among other things, the opportunity for every child to be elected to some position of responsibility among those who are his peers. The fifteen-year-old prefects of the secondary modern school will have a dignity and sense of responsibility not unlike that of the seventeen-year-old prefects of the grammar school: in a large multilateral school it is hard to see how the modern-school stream, who leave at fifteen, can avoid being perpetually overshadowed by the older members of the grammar school—who—let us be honest and face the facts—will also be much abler. In some rural areas, however, where the very scantiness of school population is the administrator's problem, and where full-blooded multi-lateralism cannot produce a school of more than 400 pupils the advantages of amalgamation may outweigh the disadvantages. Indeed, some experiments with rural *bi*lateral schools—in which the variation of pupil ability is not so great—seem to have been well worth while. But always there remains the danger that minority academic talent will get less than its due—to the nation's impoverishment.

Yet, if our aim—sociological rather than educational—be to create as in the Scandinavian democracies a nation in which differences of social status do not impose high economic or other barriers between man and man, then we would do well to reflect upon the educational systems which have been built up in those countries during over a century of compulsory education.

Firstly, we should note that in those countries it is *not* considered necessary, for national homogeneity, to keep all pupils at the secondary stage in the same building, on the same school campus, or even in the same town. Education suited to abilities and aptitudes is available for all and university education is free to all those who qualify for admission. But what *is* considered necessary is that the bulk of the children shall be educated in the same *primary* schools, and in Norway the children of the Crown Prince have attended an ordinary State primary school on the outskirts of Oslo. Where class barriers are created by different schooling it is much more likely that they take their origin from separation in early years, before differences of taste and aptitude have advanced far. Before, however, the majority of the middle class of any nation will send their children to State primary schools those schools must be so good that private ones can offer little if any advantage. Here, clearly enough, is the field to which those who wish to build our multilateral schools of 2,000 pupils would do better to devote their energies. There is no gainsaying that it is primary education which plays

Cinderella to her ugly sisters, multilateral and comprehensive, in English education to-day. Classes in primary schools are too large, which makes it difficult to recruit teachers: teachers are too few, which makes it difficult to make classes smaller. One looks back with some bitterness to those inter-war years when thousands of would-be teachers could find no posts and thousands of would-be builders could find no work. In Norway no class may in any circumstances contain more than 30 pupils and if a school contain more than 35 pupils it must be broken into at least three classes. This is not the time to enlarge upon all the shortcomings of our State primary education, but it should be said openly and plainly that our weaknesses in primary education constitute a serious leak in our educational vessel. What is more, they encourage the existence of a large number of little private schools where, if physical amenities are better, and class numbers smaller, and handling of children more friendly in consequence, the actual teaching itself leaves much to be desired and talent therefore goes to waste.

This phenomenon of the continued existence and, in certain directions, growth of private education since the 1944 Education Act is one very worthy of our attention. Mr. Wolfenden points out that, speaking generally and with notable exceptions where local education authorities have been far-seeing, the position of the grammar school has been weakened administratively. To this one must add that the financial status of the graduate teacher has been considerably weakened relatively to his non-graduate brother, and the great disparity between the financial rewards of a graduate in medicine, dentistry, scientific industry on the one hand and in education on the other is creating a series of problems, the progeny of which will still be giving us national headaches 10 years hence. Indeed, feeling within the grammar schools was so high a year or two back that a booklet entitled *The Threat to the Grammar Schools* was produced by the Incorporated Association of Headmasters. Since that time common sense has begun to reassert itself, and even the lowest levellers are coming to see that intellectual standards are not without significance in the attempt to preserve merely *physical* standards of life. But meanwhile, especially in the mathematical and scientific subjects, the best graduates have tended to be snatched up by the independent schools. To-day, despite the devastatingly heavy taxation, these independent schools, with their high fees, have, nevertheless, long waiting lists. The restrictions upon the freedom of the grammar schools and their governors, the fitting of them into a financial administrative pattern, often with a staffing ratio inadequate for a wide range of sixth-form alternative studies, all these things have encouraged parents to make sacrifices which are perhaps incommensurate in order to send their sons and daughters to independent schools, or to schools in receipt of Direct Grant where fees by parents are still payable and where staffing ratios and staff salaries are often more generous. So, in effect, class stratification in secondary education has been accentuated, rather than diminished by the administrative changes since 1944. Before the war the ordinary maintained or locally aided grammar school was a community in which boys or girls of many strata of society lived and worked happily side by side with personal qualities rather than parental income as the standard by which they were judged. To-day the extent to which this holds is more limited; maintained and aided grammar schools now contain few pupils who come from any class above the lower middle.

The exclusion from grammar school education of those who fail the selection tests of local authorities and of Direct-Grant schools has encouraged the development of private schools offering an education on grammar school, rather than modern school, lines, some of these schools being partly confessional. It is quite possible that parents who commit their 'failed grammar school' offspring to such studies are not really conferring a boon upon them. But their sturdy independence refuses to be persuaded and when some of these rejected children eventually pass in two or three subjects of the General Certificate of Education, the parents will make long noses at the local education authority, swell out their chests and say 'I *knew* no child of mine could be a failure'. We may have some sympathy with the officers of the local education authority regarding the difficult role which they are called upon to play. Yet with all the sympathy in the world one cannot acquit them of being the willing instrument, in many cases, for weakening the position of the grammar schools. Some of them, too, in the passion for administrative tidiness come to interpret education not as the influence of mind upon mind, but in terms of so many pupils in so many desks for so many hours in so many days of terms which now must be of the same length for grammar schools and secondary modern schools. This irrespective of the fact that the latter (modern schools) have no homework, very few extra curricular activities, never any Saturday school and that many grammar school pupils leave school three years later than those of the modern school and are students rather than schoolboys.

Moreover, we must, with Mr. Wolfenden, protest against the assumption that the administrator is a more important man than the headmaster, that 'ability to handle details and write clear, logical and convincing reports' (quoted from an official document) is more valuable than the capacity to teach with inspiration:

> To breathe the enlivening spirit and to fix
> The generous purpose in the glowing breast.

Yet we shall almost inevitably retain this false valuation until the system whereby educational administrators are recruited is modified. Looking at the matter from first principles one would assume that the essential experience of a future educational administrator would include:

(a) considerable knowledge of children as a result of teaching in several different types of school;

(b) considerable understanding of parents as a result of acting as head of a school;

(c) considerable experience of the needs and points of view of teachers;

(d) some administrative experience in education proper.

And there are few better ways of gaining this last than by running a school. One would suppose, therefore, that in this country, as in the U.S.A., recruitment for administrative work serving the needs of scores or hundreds of schools would in general be made from heads of schools. In actual practice this is a very rare occurrence since the advertisements for the higher administrative positions almost invariably demand previous experience in the same field. This experience can only be gained by entering administration at a salary level which is in general below that of heads of secondary schools. As a result there are cases of administrators who themselves have had as little as two years' teaching experience and that in only one type of school and without having held any position of special responsibility in that school. Indeed, we sometimes find that teaching experience in a school is not regarded as essential for an administrative post under a local authority. The following advertisement appeared in *The Times* of 6 February 1948:

. . . shire Education Committee. Applications are invited for appointments as ADMINISTRATIVE ASSISTANTS. Candidates should have a good honours degree; teaching experience desirable but not essential.

Mr. Wolfenden claims that sometimes such posts are filled by men who should be dubbed 'failed schoolmaster'. It is still worse when they are filled by men who have not even tried. We cannot expect that headmasters will take kindly to the questionnaires and regulations sent to them by people for whom they can have little professional respect. They have every right to say with Cassius: 'I had as lief not be as live to be In awe of such a thing as I myself.' What are they to say when they are asked to be in awe of men whom they cannot in justice regard as even their equals, professionally?

The right to criticize in this manner implies the duty of indicating a possible method of reform. Let us therefore put forward the firm suggestion that local education authorities should start to appoint, at high level in the administrative hierarchy, a number of men and women who have shown themselves successful as heads of schools. This would surely do much to increase friendly liaison between the schools and the administration. If we have reached an era when public funds and public control have a greater part to play in education, it is essential that the machinery shall run with the smoothness of a well-oiled dynamo.

There is, incidentally, another field where headmasters and headmistresses should be regarded as ideal candidates for appointment; namely in all levels of teacher training. With a few notable exceptions, however, the posts are advertised at salaries well below those of heads of secondary schools and so it is the subject specialist who tends to be appointed. And this at a time when it is men and women who have gone beyond their specialism and can help to break down the barriers between the divisions of knowledge who are particularly needed.

Yet there are further advantages in the transfer of heads. Within fifteen years most heads have made their essential contribution to the life of a school. They have brought about those changes which they desired, they have added the new activities which they deemed important and the time has come for them to seek new work to perform, especially work for which their experience has peculiarly fitted them. Public school headmasters may become bishops, deans, and vice-chancellors, but there are very few openings for the heads of grammar schools and secondary modern schools. In these circumstances it is easy for heads to become unwitting obstacles to change. Moreover, happiness in the teaching profession as a whole demands an adequate number of opportunities of responsibility and leadership for the younger men and women. Incidentally one may note that if multilateral schools become common the number of headships will be seriously reduced. But, whatever the situation, it is desirable that there should be more opportunities for experienced and successful heads of schools to make new contributions to the community's welfare.

A matter which has recently loomed large in the minds of headmasters and headmistresses is the recommendation of the Secondary Schools Examination Council that candidates should not be allowed to enter for the General Certificate of Education before a certain age. Mr. Wolfenden has strongly criticized the action of the Minister of Education in accepting this recommendation and he has had the support of many colleagues. On the other hand the new examination does give schools a much greater freedom than they have ever had to adapt the curriculum to the pupil. So education can be made a process of intellectual growth rather than, as the extinct School Certificate too often made it, in the past, a cramming process preparatory to successful regurgitation. Nor need bright pupils be kept back by the minimum age limit if only a variety of courses at different levels in each subject can be provided for pupils nearing certificate age. Whether, however, schools will be able to provide such variety depends entirely upon their staffing ratio. Most of the independent public schools have far fewer pupils per member of staff than the grammar schools and so can take the strain better, especially as they are not prevented from appointing more staff if they decide to do so. But the maintained and aided grammar schools are in a different plight and among these the small ones will be the hardest hit of all unless the local education authorities agree to much more generous staffing This is a point which seems as yet not to have been properly grasped. While some of the larger authorities are generous in counting sixth-form pupils as two units each for calculating staffing ratios, it will probably be necessary for pupils over school-leaving age to count as more than two units in all but the largest schools if the reforms intended are to be achieved. It is to be hoped therefore that the Minister, having used his powers to override the wishes of many of the profession, will also use them to stimulate local education authorities to play their part in implementing the new regulations.

Some educationists, in their opposition to external control, go so far as to urge that the profession as a whole should have the last word on all that concerns the life of the school. This is a dangerous position, which would probably have negated most of the developments which properly constituted advisory bodies have set on foot during the past fifty years. In fact, educational history does not support the view that the teaching profession has always known best regarding the true needs of children. One only has to go back less than two centuries to find almost the whole teaching profession of a country united in condemnation of the opinions of a writer whose views have been gradually achieving world-wide vindication ever since—the writer was Jean-Jacques Rousseau. Let us quote—in rather free translation—part of his attack on the schoolmasters of his time and of centuries before that:

They have no understanding of childhood: building on the false assumptions of the profession they go blundering on from one error to another. Even the wisest of them, though they try to discover what things are important for man to know, do not consider whether children are, in fact, capable of assimilating this knowledge. They expect to find manhood during childhood; they deny that childhood has any rights of its own.

It was this belief on the part of most pedagogues that childhood was merely a reprehensible interlude between birth and maturity that left the mark of school-day miseries upon the early years of countless millions of children.

Professor Knight's reference to the scientific discoveries which are still changing our pedagogical attitudes should serve as a further reminder that we as a profession are not yet justified in claiming the right to the final decisions of educational policies. Recently, however, at a conference of politically minded teachers in the midlands, a resolution was passed urging that 'teaching must become a self-governing profession, controlling the admission to the profession and *defining the pattern of the educational development of society*'. We must look carefully at the last few words—'defining the pattern of the educational development of society'—for surely this is one of the most arrogant claims that any group of society could put forward. Most of us would utterly repudiate such a claim for our profession, and in support of our attitude might quote words used by Professor Butterfield in one of his broadcasts on 'Christianity and History'. 'In the kind of world that I see in history', he said, 'there is one sin that locks people up in all their other sins and fastens men and nations more tightly than ever in their predicaments, namely the sin of self-righteousness.'

Having entered upon a little professional self-examination

perhaps we may continue the investigation a little farther and ask ourselves what are the greatest shortcomings of teachers to-day? We may be too near to judge, but many would suggest that we suffer most from pedagogical sclerosis—that hardening of the intellectual arteries which gradually reduces the flow of fresh red blood to a mere thread of scarlet. Most of us tend too soon to become routinized in our teaching, fixed in our judgements, and impervious to new ideas. But for this degeneration teachers are not wholly to blame. It is still assumed by administrators that once a man or woman has been prepared for classroom work by an education diploma or certificate, then despite a changing world little else is required. It is supposed that the teacher has received sufficient academic charge to keep him going for forty years, or even longer. It is true that there are short refresher courses which teachers may attend in the school vacations. But they must meet most of the costs themselves—and this is a task beyond the financial powers of most middle-aged men with families. Also some local education authorities arrange week-end courses and non-residential one-day schools. These are all to the good, and one wants to see them multiplied a hundred-fold. But even so they cannot provide that real refreshment which comes from returning to study and bringing oneself again up to date in one's special subjects, or, in the case of graduates, getting near again to the frontiers of knowledge and the thrill of research. Surely no man or woman should be asked to teach for more than twenty years without being given the opportunity of at least three months of study or other enriching experience as a half-time refreshment in a lifetime's work? Still more acutely will this need be felt ten years hence by the many thousands of 'emergency trained' teachers. Though these men and women have a very high sense of vocation, many are handicapped by an inadequate or somewhat distant background of general education. This problem of keeping the teaching profession abreast of life in the rapidly changing world of the second half of the twentieth century is one which has not yet been properly faced anywhere in the world though several countries are in advance of our own. 'Learning' says Harold Butler 'always lags a generation behind life.' So long as this is true ever-increasing expenditure on what Whitehead calls 'inert knowledge' will be superb folly.

With the decline in church-going and with the commercialization of so many influences which affect both public taste and judgement, the school-teacher has greater responsibilities than ever thrust upon him. If he cannot influence the choice of leisure occupations of our future citizens, in a world of much increased leisure, or increase the sense of social responsibility, in a nation where social inter-dependence becomes more absolute, the future may be disturbing. As Sir Richard Livingstone has said: 'If we have a people, only a section of which is educated, with the rest having nothing better to do with their leisure than the cinema, the football pools and racing, then it is hardly worth having a democracy at all.' Particularly in the field of adult education there is need for advance in which a great part must be played in evenings by graduate schoolmasters. Most of all, in the internationally inter-dependent world which is rapidly taking shape before our eyes, there is need for basic mutual understanding among the peoples of western democracies. Without this any hope of constructive advance towards world harmony, or even the alternative of united resistance against aggression, is doomed to failure. In all democratic countries, therefore, two things are urgently necessary. Firstly, the teaching profession shall be enabled to perform its important function of breaking down new thoughts and ideas which are not easily assimilable by the bulk of the people into simpler form more closely related to the concrete things of physical existence. Secondly, there must be built up a fundamental sense of accord and an inward feeling of cross-frontier solidarity with members of the teaching profession in other democracies, and even—as the future hope of the world—in countries not yet democratic by our standards.

Moreover, if it is necessary, as I believe it to be, to keep teachers from becoming narrowed in vision and antiquated in ideas, then there is no finer way of refreshing them than by interchange and contact with opposite numbers abroad. This is how Professor Bowra put it when he was advocating the formation of an international university.

An equally great need is for greater and closer contact between teachers of different countries, not merely at the highest level, but at all levels. The fundamental problems of teaching are the same everywhere and a new experience gained in one country cannot but be of service to another. As it is such contacts are extremely rare, short and confined to a few fortunate people. . . . The danger of all education is that it may become stereotyped and that what suits one generation is assumed to be suitable for another. This is not always true. A period of social change may well need methods different from those used in a period of stability, and it is important to know how new needs have been met and how far they can be met in the same way elsewhere. Therefore we need a greater contact in the first place between teachers of all kinds in different countries.

He goes on to consider what could be done and the difficulties in the way. 'None the less,' he says '. . . some scheme must be evolved by which the teachers of one country can study on the spot the methods of another country.' We know that because teachers in all countries are financially straitened, especially those with families, this can only be arranged by a willingness of governments to invest money in this work of creating international intellectual solidarity.

As Sir John Maud points out, developments in this direction are expanding, though save for the case of assistants in France —and these are *young* teachers of French, not men and women in need of refreshment—the numbers bear no relation to the size of the problem. Indeed, there is a danger that a counting of the number of countries with which a few exchanges are made may lead to a misconception of the situation and to a false sense of complacency. It is not the nature of such developments which is questioned, but their extent and their rate of expansion. Nor will the thousands of *holidays* abroad, in which teachers have their share, contribute very much to the purposes in mind: such things do not meet Professor Bowra's point about studying on the spot the methods of another country, nor do they provide that length of contact without which enriching understanding cannot grow.

As for teachers acting as foci of a new world outlook, let us see what has been done to help teachers in this country, since the war, to play their part. We find that among the scores of summer courses for teachers arranged in England by our Ministry of Education not *one* has dealt with any aspect of international affairs or the United Nations. If anyone suspect that the courses tend to be confined to the standard school subjects, an examination of the programmes will show a remarkable range of taste extending from bacon-curing for the Rabelaisian to the arrangement of flowers for the deliciously aesthetic.

Yet the British contribution to the development of constructive international thought since the war is no mean one and its cradling of Unesco must rank highly in this respect. Considering the brief span of its existence and the many difficulties that have had to be overcome, the total effect of Unesco upon the world's thought has been quite impressive and will become more so. But in recounting progress and in the justifiable satisfaction that results, there is always the danger that we fail equally to tot up the balance of the opposing forces. Particularly we may forget that sense of urgency which Sir Raymond Priestley and A. J. Toynbee have urged upon us. When all our applause for Unesco's achievement is over, there still arises the question—is this adequate? In spite of the fundamental education work possible under the technical assistance plan surely the right answer was that given by the Director-General Dr. Torres Bodet when he said in September 1949 'it would be wrong to give the impression that the Education programme, on the scale on which it is now being conducted, is going far towards meeting the vast educational problems of the world'. He went on to show that, because of shortage of funds, Unesco is afraid to press its requests for information even in restricted fields, lest the meagre staff should be overwhelmed by the replies that would result. If anyone should wonder how and why these things should be, let him turn to the records of Unesco's Preparatory Conference in 1946. There he will find that delegates agreed that if the budget for the first year were less than $7,500,000, the programme would be crippled. They therefore recommended a budget of $7,611,139.

At the same time they unanimously agreed, and recorded this view, that though so small a budget was justified in the first year, when only a beginning would be made in many of the projects, yet 'the programme and the budget should show a high rate of expansion during the first years of its operation'. Yet year after year the budget has been cut, and in the fourth year of Unesco's existence, its budget was limited to some $8,000,000, a sum which, before devaluation, was less for the educational, scientific, and cultural exchange of fifty nations, than was spent by the British Council in equivalent work for one nation. This is not the place to discuss the reasons, sound or unsound, far-sighted or short-sighted, logical or illogical, which led the United Kingdom in three years out of four to play a prominent part in the reduction of Unesco's budget.

The very difficulty of Unesco finding suitable personnel may alone have completely justified the policy of holding down Unesco's expenditure. But what is disturbing—or should be—is that the British public knows so little of Unesco's work and purposes that the financial policies of the United Kingdom delegation receive no comment in the press.

It has proved convenient to leave to this stage our consideration of the application of education to industry and to industrial relations. Dr. Revans, in dealing with this subject, makes a closely reasoned appeal for great extension of the policy of consultation between management and workers. He emphasizes, however, that there can be no hope of success in such consultation unless both management and workers be completely honest and sincere; there must be no half-truths, no withholding of information but an honourable attempt on both sides to face a common problem and to evolve means of solving it. This, Dr. Revans thinks, might justifiably be regarded as an educative process, even though it involves few of the normal educational techniques and takes us into fields of applied psychology which have scarcely been properly mapped. Regarding technical education he expresses the view that all the basic skills of technology should be taught in technical schools and he gives good reasons why the production shop is not a suitable place for acquiring such forms of knowledge. This is an extremely important matter on which the same opinion is held by the Vice-Chancellor of Leeds. 'Technical skills', says Mr. Morris, 'must be general and not related to specific machines.'

This principle has been largely adopted on the Continent, notably in French post-war technical education. Here the apprenticeship centres, institutions which are a hybrid between school and factory, constitute one of the most exciting experiments of twentieth-century education. Two points in particular link them with the thought of Dr. Revans. Firstly, every apprenticeship centre is governed by its own committee consisting of equal numbers of trade-union representatives, employers, and educationists. Secondly, about one-third of the forty hours of weekly attendance is devoted to specialized liberal studies. The word 'specialized' is here used to indicate that these are not *intended* to be the ordinary secondary-school subjects treated in the ordinary secondary-school manner, too often unrelated to the life of the pupil. On the contrary the attempt is made to link them with the technical studies which form the bait, so that the unsuspecting pupil swallows not merely the bait but hook and sinker as well.

This concession to the desire of the average young person between the ages of fourteen and eighteen to get to grips with life has much to justify it. Schoolmasters and schoolmistresses too often seem to resent the desire of the adolescent to grow up, to achieve independence, to flaunt the pipe of manhood and the cigarette of womanhood before the world. *In statu pupillarii* is a blessed phrase that slips lightly off the tongue of the don, but sometimes has the flavour of vinegar in the mouth of the undergraduate. Most of us would maintain the principle in the very attenuated form in which it still exists in English universities. But there is an unnatural childishness which is demanded of most adolescents at school, particularly in some boarding-schools. As a result there is a great deal of frustration among adolescents in this country and futile wastage of energy. Nor is this phenomenon confined to the United Kingdom. Quite recently an American professor of education pointed out to an Oxford audience that, whereas fifty years ago American youths of eighteen were opening up new farmland and new industries in the Middle West, marrying at twenty and founding sturdy families, to-day thousands of such young men in high schools are conducted by a schoolmistress only a few years their senior, to study industry by visiting the local jam factory. It is a good thing to be brought sometimes face to face with such grisly warnings.

Let us therefore find no professional shame in asking for a great extension in this country of technical education which shall liberalize as well as technicize the student and which, as in France, shall be free from the typical schoolteacher-pupil relationship. It should recognize, with approval, the desire of every well-constituted young man to be about his business and to prepare himself a position in life, where, as a result of some professional or craft skill, some technical knowledge or experience, he can look the world in the face confident of his ability—in a rational world—to earn his living by contributing to one of the needs of society.

No doubt there are some who will disagree very strongly with this plea for treating adolescents a little more like adults. To these one may reply by quoting Shakespeare—always a sound move in argument. When Shakespeare divided a man's life into its seven ages he discerned no such phase as we in this country to-day call 'the young person', no such stage as the Americans call 'the teen age' no such being as the 'bobby soxer'. As Shakespeare saw the progression the next part played after that of the schoolboy was that of the lover—very definitely a matter of getting to grips with life.

As for philosophy, Professor Reid has made clear the need for much more thought on fundamentals and for leavening biology, psychology, sociology, and kindred sciences with philosophical wisdom. Indeed, according to some thinkers it is precisely because philosophy has failed to take note of and understand scientific advance that humanity finds itself to-day on the brink of the abyss. Many of us think, however, with Professor Reid that it is the religious approach rather than the philosophic of which the world stands in need. Nevertheless, a quotation from Bernard Lovell, a Manchester University physicist, helps to link Professor Reid's thoughts with those of Dr. Revans. Lovell writes:

The void between man's code of behaviour and the material powers which science and technology have placed in his hands is a direct result of the sterility of philosophy in the face of the dynamic advance of science. The progress of scientific discovery has been cumulative, but in each age the philosophers wrestle afresh with the eternal values so that, as Schweitzer remarks '. . . in the sphere of ethics, we live in a town full of ruins, in which one generation builds for itself here and another there, what is absolutely necessary'.

Of the need for that type of reflection upon life which is in the broad sense philosophical there can, however, be no doubt. The need for this in education is evidently supreme since in the absence of clearly visualized ends, school-teachers are like those who, in the words of George Santayana, 'redouble their efforts the more they lose sight of their objective'.

At what stage should the philosophical thinking begin? Some say that philosophy should begin in the sixth forms of grammar schools. But we have Plato's warning against teaching it to boys. 'Those who study philosophy at all do it in this way, when they are just emerged from boyhood . . . and in after years if they ever accept an invitation to listen to a philosophical discussion, they are quite proud of themselves, for they look upon it as a mere pastime.' Others say that it should form a part of every university course. If special philosophical courses, quite distinct from those of the honours schools in the subject, could be arranged, as Professor Reid suggests, for association with all other subjects, then a great step forward might be made.

But if teachers are ever to have, as I have claimed for them, at least one long period of break from output, a period for travel, or reflection, or study, or for all three, then clearly here is an ideal time for further philosophy. By that stage of life—after some ten years or more of teaching—a man or woman has generally tasted enough both of joys and sorrows to begin to see life with a sense of perspective. The adolescent wants to master his trade or calling, the young man who has established his professional security wants to play a vigorous part in the affairs of the community. By early middle age the man or woman is more willing to reflect and has that wider experience upon which to base his judgements. Indeed, it was at such a stage that Plato wanted his future philosopher kings to turn to the study of dialectic for which they could not be sufficiently mature before the age of thirty. But this suggestion is given merely by way of example. It is only *one* stage, in *one* profession among many, where philosophical studies have much to contribute. A world in which increased leisure does not lead to increased reflection and to increased concern in the higher quests of the human mind is obviously misusing its opportunities.

Whether we should go so far as to share Professor Reid's anxiety regarding those who, professing no Christian ethic, may in default adopt the views of the scientific humanists, is an open question. There may be many who, finding that their perception of things spiritual is not readily clothed in a traditional terminology which they consider outworn, prefer to maintain a silence which is misconstrued as a denial.

However this may be, we are in less speculative regions when we recall one of the passages of Mr. Morris's opening chapter. He reminded us of a not far-distant period of educational history —when, incidentally, the Christian ethic was much more upon the tongue—in which the social concept was that of a community in which a certain number of its members received a generous and liberal education while the rest of its members were compelled to work as soon as possible. If scientific humanism has helped to change that concept, and so helped to give to millions a greater opportunity of fulfilling the Christian ideal of glorifying God and enjoying Him for ever, through the development of their intellectual and spiritual powers, then its part has not been entirely negative.

Perhaps in this quest for truth it is not the position at which one arrives that must be counted for virtue, but the whole-hearted and utter surrender of oneself in that search.